PRAISE FOR THE HITCHHIKER'S GUIDE TO THE *Canva* CLASSROOM

DANAE ACKER
DIGITAL INTEGRATION SPECIALIST

"This Hitchhiker's Guide to the Canva Classroom will inspire you in so many ways. Your creative side is about to explode! If you are new to Canva or even a guru, this guide is for you!"

MICHAEL COHEN
DESIGNER, PROBLEM SOLVER, STORYTELLER

"In this hitchhikers guide, Amanda shows you how to leverage Canva to bring learning to life. Through creative lessons, her own examples, and those of educators the world over, she showcases just how powerful technology can be when exploring ways to foster meaningful teaching and learning."

ERIC CURTS
TECH INTEGRATIONIST

"So have you wanted to use Canva, but didn't know where to start? Don't panic! Amanda Fox has provided the ultimate guide with "The Canva Classroom". This book covers everything you need to know about Canva features, integrations, and templates, along with the pedagogy behind designing impactful learning experiences for your students."

NADINE GILKISON
SPECIALIST FRANKLIN TOWNSHIP SCHOOLS

"When I think of Canva graphic design comes to mind instantly...posters, presentations, social media. Amanda's take on utilizing everything Canva has to offer for adults AND students in the classroom has my brain churning with ideas to implement immediately! The fact that she also includes templates to jump start your journey makes this the complete package. Well done!"

PRAISE FOR THE HITCHHIKER'S GUIDE TO THE *Canva* CLASSROOM

TARA HANNON
MEDIA SPECIALIST

"The Hitchhiker's Guide to the Canva Classroom is a must have book that all educators need to add to their tech toolbox. This book provides templates, design techniques, and specific how-to instructions that will bring your lessons to the next level. This book not only aligns Canva designs with educational frameworks we are already using in the classroom, but it also shows how we can integrate Canva with other edu apps. The best part? You do not need any graphic design experience to create engaging and inclusive lessons… all you need is this book!"

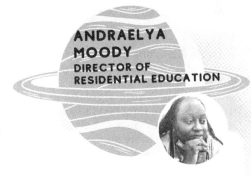

ANDRAELYA MOODY
DIRECTOR OF RESIDENTIAL EDUCATION

"Amanda and I went to school together from kindergarten to graduation and I'm proud to see her publish such an amazing work that is intentional in message and captures the heart of teachers. I wish our teachers had access to Canva and this guide as a resource to create engaging learning content!"

RYAN READ
HS TEACHER

"Amanda Fox has written a must-read, but also a fun and creative journey into the world of Canva from classroom teachers to administration. Read this book!"

TISHA RICHMOND
CANVA CONSULTANT

"Amanda is a creative genius! Whether you are a Canva for education beginner or a pro, you will devour The Canva Classroom and come away with tons of ideas and inspiration! Get out your sticky notes and highlighters…this is a book that you will refer to often to take your lessons to infinity and beyond!"

PRAISE FOR THE HITCHHIKER'S GUIDE TO THE *Canva* CLASSROOM

BRETT SALAKAS
HP EDUCATION AMBASSDOR

"Amanda Fox is one of the most influential educators in the world today. Her inspiring ideas first reached Australian shores several years ago. Her latest book, 'The Hitchhiker's Guide to the Canva Classroom' does not disappoint! It is filled with the same quality, fun and practicality that Amanda has become known for."

BRAD & ALAINA WEINSTEIN
TEACHERGOALS

"The Hitchhiker's Guide to the Canva Classroom is a fantastic addition to your professional learning shelf. If you think this book is amazing, you should check out her course on www.teachergoals.com/courses/. The course is everything you need to launch Canva in your classroom!"

LIKE THE BOOK AND WANT TO LEAVE SOME OUT OF THIS WORLD PRAISE? SCAN THE QR CODE TO GET THIS REVIEW TEMPLATE. WRITE YOUR REVIEW, ADD YOUR PHOTO AND POST IT TO SOCIAL MEDIA!

42+

ULTIMATE ANSWERS TO TEMPLATES THAT ROCKET STUDENT ENGAGEMENT

THE
Canva
CLASSROOM

FOREWORD BY SCOTT NUNES, DISTRICT ENGAGEMENT ADVOCATE AT *Canva*

AMANDA FOX

The Hitchhiker's Guide to the Canva Classroom

Published by TeacherGoals Publishing, LLC, Beech Grove, IN
www.teachergoals.com

Cover and Interior Design by Amanda Fox

Library of Congress Control Number: 2022906806
Paperback ISBN: 978-1-959419-00-6
Ebook/Kindle ASBN: B09XLNFBRK

First Printing April 2022
Reprint January 2023

Canva is a trademark of Canva Pty Ltd.

The Canva Classroom is an independent publication and has not been authorized, sponsored, or otherwise approved by Canva Pty Ltd.

TEACHERGOALS
PUBLISHING

DEDICATION

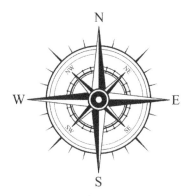

To my kiddos, Rowan, Bridgit, Connor, and Finnick: thank you for being my compass and guiding me through life as much as I try to guide you. To my Mimi who has been my biggest cheerleader in life.

To all of the wonderful teachers who have supported me through the years, and to the wonderful teachers that taught me, especially Ms. Muldrew, Mr. Holloway, Dr. Jamison, and Mrs. Shepherd.

And to my loving husband, Patrick, who puts up with the glow of a computer through the night. 459.

GALAXY OF CONTENTS

DESTINATION 6

DESTINATION 5

DESTINATION 4

 COURSES *by* TEACHERGOALS

REGISTER NOW!

www.teachergoals.com/canvaclassroomcourse

Don't panic! Relax, because this course, based on *The Canva Classroom* book is designed as an educator's design guide to creating meaningful student tasks and projects using the Canva design platform. Each module is designed to help you fully leverage the Canva platform with the goal of embracing creativity, student voice, collaboration, critical thinking, and community. With over 8 hours of video enhanced instruction you are guaranteed to walk away a Canva pro!

01 Canva for Education Set Up

02 Designing For Inclusivity: UbD and UDL

03 Designing for Depth of Knowledge

04 Using Canva to Enhance Instruction

05 Canva Tips, Hacks, and Tricks

06 Canva App Integrations and App Smashing

07 Creating a Canva Brand Kit

08 Creating Learning Experiences in Canva

09 Feedback, Assessment, and Folders

10 Social Media and Community Building

PARTICIPANTS WILL:

- Learn how to set up a Canva Classroom and register for the Canva Education Dashboard.
- Explore pedagogical foundations such as Depth of Knowledge, Universal Design Framework, Backwards Design.
- Explore over 10 ways to app smash with Canva and be given examples.
- Complete learning tasks demonstrating understanding of Canva feature and functions.
- Experience the platform from a student perspective.
- Create a classroom, school, or district brand kit.
- Design an interactive lesson using Canva and its integrated functions.
- Learn how to organize folders, follow creators, and save elements.
- Explore multiple ways to provide feedback and assessment using Canva.
- Learn how to use Canva to engage socially and build a global PLN.
- Interact with other Canva Educators in the FB Group.

PROFESSIONAL DEVELOPMENT OFFERINGS

For more information on booking Amanda for book readings, summer camps, keynotes, workshops, design thinking led sessions, or video conferencing/virtual book readings with your class or school, go to Teachergoals.com. If you are looking for an asynchronous PD credited course check out her Canva Classroom online offering through TeacherGoals.com/courses. Amanda can customize and tailor school and district trainings to fit your specific need as well.

@ AMANDAFOXSTEM

SESSIONS AND WORKSHOPS

CANVA VISION: VIDEO CREATION FOR MULTIVERSE INSTRUCTION

DOK PUNCHOUT: TKO DOK WITH CANVA

THE CANVA CLASSROOM VIRTUAL COURSE BY TEACHERGOALS

OH SNAP: APP SMASHING IN THE CANVA UNIVERSE

THE HITCHHIKER'S GUIDE TO THE CANVA CLASSROOM

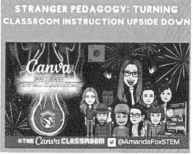

STRANGER PEDAGOGY: TURNING CLASSROOM INSTRUCTION UPSIDE DOWN

TEACHERGOALS.COM/PD   CONTACT@TEACHERGOALS.COM

COMPREHENSIVE CHART OF CANVA EXAMPLES AND TEMPLATES

*DOK=Depth of Knowledge

Template	DOK 1	DOK 2	DOK 3	DOK 4	Page #
Jeopardy Template	x				24
Iron Chef Template		x			24
Lego Masters Template			x		24
Shark Tank Template				x	24
Single Lesson Template	n/a	n/a	n/a	n/a	31
Weekly Lesson Template	n/a	n/a	n/a	n/a	32
Unit Lesson Template	n/a	n/a	n/a	n/a	33
Daily Agenda Template	n/a	n/a	n/a	n/a	34
Design Principles Poster Template	n/a	n/a	n/a	n/a	37
Worst Preso Ever Template		x			42
10 C's of Canva Poster	n/a	n/a	n/a	n/a	47
Stranger Things Vocabulary Template		x			67
Google Classroom Header	n/a	n/a	n/a	n/a	72
Club Flyer Template	n/a	n/a	n/a	n/a	72
Bathroom Sign Out QR Code Example	n/a	n/a	n/a	n/a	72
Newsletter to Parent Example	n/a	n/a	n/a	n/a	72
Hyperdoc Parts of Speech			x		73

Template	DOK 1	DOK 2	DOK 3	DOK 4	Page #
Democracy Flipped Lecture		x			74
Audio/Visual Instructions Example	n/a	n/a	n/a	n/a	74
Simple Machines Scavenger Hunt		x			76
Bitmoji: The Socratic Raven			x		77
Bitmoji CR: Meet the Teacher	n/a	n/a	n/a	n/a	77
Virtual Escape Room Example			x		80
Canva Digital Breakout Template			x		80
Edgar Alan Poe Breakout w/ Canva			x		81
Digital Citizenship Breakout			x		81
Mystery Cards Template	n/a	n/a	n/a	n/a	83
Magic Shortcuts Poster	n/a	n/a	n/a	n/a	84
Learning Stations Example				x	87
Comic Strip Vocabulary Template		x			93
Digital Scratch Off Ticket Template	n/a	n/a	n/a	n/a	97
Emoji Exit Ticket Template	x				107
STEM Capeless Crusaders Podcast				x	109
Peardeck Templates		x	x		110
The Canva Classroom Flipgrid Background		x			111

Template	DOK 1	DOK 2	DOK 3	DOK 4	Page #
Wonderopolis Poster Template		x			114
Student Certificates	n/a	n/a	n/a	n/a	115
Jam Board Template		x			116
Wakelet Header	n/a	n/a	n/a	n/a	117
Hamilton Student Workbook (GD)				x	117
Canva + Genially Example		x			121
Canva + Classroomscreen Example			x		121
Sketchnote Examples		x			126
Stranger Word Matrix Template		x			133
Mind Frayer Model Template		x			135
Shades of Meaning Templates			x		137
Wordle Template		x			139
Hexagonal Thinking Template			x		141
Magnetic Poetry Template			x		144
Black Out Poetry Template			x		146
The Masked Singer Template				x	148
One Pager Assignment				x	150
Instagram Template			x		154

Template	DOK 1	DOK 2	DOK 3	DOK 4	Page #
Amazon Book Review Template		x			156
Facebook Template		x			157
Pinterest Template		x			158
Youtube Template		x			159
TikTok Template		x			160
Social Calendar Template		x			161
Fake Text Template		x			162
Food Saga Unit (Book Creator)				x	164
Podcast Unit Template (Book Creator)				x	169
Wanted! Shapes (Book Creator)			x		173
Manifest Destiny Unit Template (BC)				x	177
Literature Circles Template				x	181
KWL Template	x				186
Cornell Notes Template	x				187
Smart Goals Template	x				188
Venn Diagram Template		x			189
Design Thinking Template				x	190
Stop Motion Animation Template			x		192

Template	DOK 1	DOK 2	DOK 3	DOK 4	Page #
Black History Month Template		x			194
March Mathness Template		x			197
Pizza Fractions Brochure Template			x		199
Telling Time Template		x			201
Graphing Parabolas Template		x			203
Handwriting Template	x				206
Sentence Construction Template		x			208
Digital Coding Template		x			210
Global Goals Template				x	213
Edtech Roundup Template	n/a	n/a	n/a	n/a	230

TO ACCESS ALL THE TEMPLATES IN THE BOOK, SCAN THE QR CODE OR GO TO THE WEBSITE BELOW.

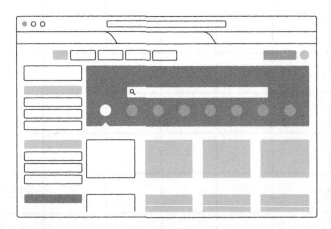

SCAN ME

WWW.TEACHERGOALS.COM/CANVATEMPLATES

**Scott Nunes,
District Engagement Advocate
@Canva**

FOREWORD

As I write my own book, I reflect on all I have learned from Amanda's shares on The Canva Classroom. After witnessing all of the work that goes into a well-thought-out project like this, I am truly inspired and know you will be too. She hustled to make this happen! Talk about hustle, this gal has a bit and then some! Eric Thomas, a well-known motivational speaker, has a talk titled, 'How Bad Do You Want It?' In it, he illustrates the barriers to wanting something and making it happen. I have witnessed Amanda sacrifice and push past numerous barriers and persist in her dedication to bringing this work to fruition. When she asked if I would write the foreword, not only was, I honored, but I knew I had to be a part of something bigger than me. As we chatted throughout the writing process and content development—sometimes into the wee hours of the day— I knew Amanda, like me, understood that Canva is unlike anything out there in that it stands alone in what it sets out to do: It makes everyone that uses it look good, and it does it with ease.

You do not need to be a freelance graphic designer of 20-plus years, like me, to create like a pro! In fact, Canva is so easy that students of all ages and abilities can unlock the engaging possibilities held within! It is as easy as typing an idea, standard, or subject in the search bar and designing from templates or elements in Canva's ever-growing library of digital assets! With over 75 million assets to assist in the creation and articulation of ideas, solutions, and demonstrations of knowledge, the possibilities are as endless as the potential of those educators serve daily! Canva has scaled it's offering significantly over the last several years to now include amazing features like a robust background remove tool, draw tool, PDF import, and more!

As a former ELA teacher that loves PBL, UDL, and Backwards Design I am elated that Amanda put pedagogical frameworks at the core of this book. I love tech, but without proper articulation and formulation of a plan to link this great communications tool to standards or areas of mastery—it is simply just something fun—which honestly, at times, is pretty cool too, but cannot be the modus operandi. This book hones in on identifying key targets in lesson development early, which builds a foundation of content and application knowledge.

Amanda demonstrates that Canva is a versatile design tool for creating lessons, activities, and environments that genuinely drive student interest and engagement. Using sound pedagogical frameworks, the book models what a solid lesson should look like and demonstrates how to challenge students of all abilities. The inclusion of Webb's Depth of Knowledge in the lesson design is solid gold! Readers can quickly have a well-structured lesson right away and not have to spend hours planning and instead can refocus that time. Maybe even have a little fun with Canva and lesson design/planning! I wish I had this as a new teacher! These are so good that I plan on using this book as a primer for my team at Canva!

Additionally, Amanda includes a 10 C's to the Canva Classroom Framework that simply stuns and launches students beyond standard learning scenarios into an interstellar path of learning possibilities. The framework is built on the foundation of the 4Cs, which prepares students for real-world dynamics and fosters connections from in-class experiences beyond the walls of the classroom. Six additional C's skyrocket the connections, my absolute favorite being the inclusion of culture. It devours the status quo and propels learners of all abilities to go beyond what others only dream possible. I like to say when it comes to Canva: "If you can dream it, you can create it!" These critical pedagogical constructs keep the focus on student voice and choice throughout the engaged learning experience! Amanda clearly illustrates the effectiveness of this powerful design tool in the classroom to activate student and educator potential in such an intuitive way.

I implore you not only to buy and read this book but to share it with others! If you want to improve your workflow, save time, improve your lessons, exceed your goals, dream big, and bring those dreams to life, then this book is for you. If you are still tired from a pandemic that just won't quit, this book is for you. If you are struggling and need help, this book is for you too. And if you just want to look good and share things that make you look like you spent all night doing it, then Canva and this book are for you! It serves as a great reference to come back to when you need a bit of inspiration or pep in your step when it comes to instructional design.

Share it with your PLN, both locally and across your network, and share it with new teachers that need all of the support and resources they can get! This is an excellent addition to any induction program or book study. I know Amanda supports me in my personal goal to support educators right where they are—ready to lead, ready to discover new possibilities—I cannot wait to see how this book helps you grow your already amazing skill set!

I love educators everywhere and am confident that you will unlock new possibilities because you are simply amazing. Just be sure to tag Amanda (@AmandaFoxSTEM) and me (@MrNunesTeach) so we can celebrate your path in the Canva journey!

Scott Nunes @MrNunesteach · Feb 26
Showing some #etclove!!! Met so many great folks today!!! Thanks for letting me gush about Canva!

 1   2   20

Scott Nunes @MrNunesteach · Mar 1
Did an hour just fly by?!!!

Wow this is the fastest, deep chat in the East!

Love sharing all about pedagogy, @canva, and community building with @tishrich and @JenWomble on today's #fetcchat!!!

Jennifer Womble #FETCchat Moderator @JenWomble · Mar 1
Thank you for joining our #FETCchat
I don't want it to end!! So much to share!
Glad you could join us tonight to learn more about @Canva!
THANKS Tisha Richmond & Scott Nunes
@MrNunesteach @tishrich
Have a great week!
Keep pushing Forward for the Future of Education Technology!

Scott Nunes @MrNunesteach · Mar 2
Hey #celebrated!!! Scott Nunes former ELA teacher turned Tech Coach and now District Engagement Advocate with Canva!

About This Book

WHAT'S INSIDE

Don't panic! Relax, because this book is written as an educator's design guide to creating meaningful student tasks and projects using the Canva design platform. Matter of fact, this whole book was created in Canva to showcase the versatility of the platform! Whether you are a seasoned teacher or just starting your first year in the classroom, this book will help you create an in-class or online classroom culture that embraces creativity, student voice, collaboration, critical thinking, and community while ensuring your Canva templates facilitate inquiry and allow students to uniquely communicate their knowledge. No matter what grade, subject, or topic you teach! It's ok if you aren't familiar with The Hitchhiker's Guide to the Galaxy— we just borrowed from the theme to drive home the importance of asking good questions to inform lesson design. This book will still be a valuable journey, and with each page, I hope to open up a whole new universe of possibilities for yourself and your students. Canva is a unicorn of a tool that students will adopt in their personal and professional lives long after they leave the classroom.

HOW TO READ THIS BOOK

The guide is broken down into six main sections, or what I refer to as destinations, because we all know learning is about the journey. This book can be read cover to cover if you wish, or in parts. If you already have a Canva classroom set up you may want to skip to other parts of the book that are relevant to where you are in your Canva journey.

In Destination One, I cover my Canva origin story, how it has truly transformed my workflow, and why I believe it is such a powerful tool. I also begin to lay down the foundation of asking good questions using Norman Webb's Depth of Knowledge Framework and why design principles are important for students to become career and college ready. In Destination Two, Canva for Education is unpacked. I highlight features and functions to help you successfully set up your Canva classroom and navigate the dashboard like a pro—including how to import students and create classes and assignments. Destination Three covers best instructional strategies to teach using Canva for the in-class or virtual classroom.

Destination Four goes into detail on the features and apps that integrate with Canva, both internally and externally. Brace yourself! There is a lot! You will be leveraging integrated apps and app smashing with the best of them! Destination Five transports us to student creativity and opportunities for collaboration with template examples and student work samples. And finally, Destination Six broaches ways you can use Canva to communicate with stakeholders outside of the classroom. By the end of this journey, you will have hitchhiked your way through over 42 templates and strategies that comprise our standard repository for all knowledge and wisdom (the strategies and templates we have created) and will be summoned to add your own! We can't wait to sweep you up in a whirlwind of Canvastellar experiences that you can successfully replicate for your classroom!

Are you ready for a
THUMBS UP
Journey?

THEN THUMB OVER TO THE
NEXT PAGE!

 CONNECT WITH ME ON TWITTER

 AMANDAFOXSTEM

"THE HITCHHIKER'S GUIDE HAS ALREADY SUPPLANTED THE GREAT ENCYCLOPEDIA GALACTICA AS THE STANDARD REPOSITORY OF ALL KNOWLEDGE AND WISDOM, FOR THOUGH IT HAS MANY OMISSIONS . . . IT SCORES OVER THE OLDER, MORE PEDESTRIAN WORK IN TWO IMPORTANT RESPECTS. FIRST, IT IS SLIGHTLY CHEAPER; AND SECONDLY IT HAS THE WORDS DON'T PANIC INSCRIBED IN LARGE FRIENDLY LETTERS ON ITS COVER."

—THE FOREWORD TO THE HITCHHIKER'S GUIDE TO THE GALAXY, 1979

Destination One: Foundation of Good Design & Pedagogy

WHY 42?

HITCHHIKER'S GUIDE FOR EDUCATORS AND THE NUMBER 42

As I sit here and pen the first paragraphs of the first book in the series of "The Hitchhiker's Guide for Educators" the irony isn't lost on me that it is the 42nd anniversary of the release of Douglas Adam's popular 1979 sci-fi novel "The Hitchhiker's Guide to the Galaxy;" the work in which I pay homage to with my title. Since it's release, there has been a lot of buzz around the number 42, which was quickly adopted by geek culture, and if you have read or seen the "The Hitchhiker's Guide to the Galaxy", then you know the significance to the number; the answer to the ultimate question of life, the universe, and everything is "forty-two." There have been countless articles on whether the number has mathematical properties, historical significance, or is completely arbitrary. So...why 42?

According to the Scientific American, when Adams was asked "Why 42?" In an online group discussion, he replied, "It was a joke. It had to be a number, an ordinary, smallish number, and I chose that one. Binary representations, base thirteen, Tibetan monks are all complete nonsense. I sat at my desk, stared into the garden and thought '42 will do.' I typed it out. End of story." But there has to be some significance right?

In the book series, the manifestation of the number is not as shrouded in mystery as it is in geek culture, but instead found quite anticlimactic. In the novel, a super intelligent alien race creates a supercomputer named "Deep Thought" designed specifically to find the answer to the ultimate meaning of life.

After seven and a half million years of calculation and thought, the computer arrived at the ominous number of 42, but the answer was ultimately met with disappointment by those seeking the answer.

They realized the problem was that the initial question was ill framed, or poorly formulated; an answer is only as good as the question evokes...right? The epiphany that the answer was essentially useless led to the construction of an even larger supercomputer, the planet Earth, designed to formulate better questions to the answer, but it was in fact destroyed minutes before its ten million year task was to be completed....

Long story short, a second Earth is created after the destruction of the first, which brings us to the entrance of Arthur Dent, the story's protagonist, as he learns Earth Mark Two is in fact also about to be destroyed to make way for a hyperspace bypass. But fear not! His friend Ford Prefect masquerading as the human is actually a researcher for the Hitchhiker's Guide and he saves him with moments to spare and so here begins an interdimensional journey in time and space that is a staple in geek culture. But how does this connect to education?

"OFTEN TIMES OUR LESSONS CAN FALL SHORT DUE TO THE LACK OF WELL DEFINED OBJECTIVES AND POOR QUESTIONING TACTICS."

ASKING GOOD QUESTIONS

As Earthly inhabitants and educators we can learn a lot from this scene when it comes to designing learning experiences and objectives for our own students. I mean, in the Hitchhiker's Guide to the Galaxy, Earth was created to calculate the important questions to the ultimate answer. If that isn't the quintessence of education, then I don't know what is.

But oftentimes our lessons can fall short due to the lack of well defined objectives and poor questioning tactics. According to Forbes, "the ability to ask questions is one of the most important lifelong learning skills a student can acquire in the course of their education," and questioning as a learning strategy has a long history in traditional education going back to the Socratic method (Brodsky, 2021).

The same Forbes article goes on to state students that learn to ask their own questions are more likely to become self autonomous learners. Robert Langer, MIT innovator says, "When you're a student, you're judged by how well you answer questions, but in life, you're judged by how good your questions are." Our job as teachers is to model this process of good question asking in order to activate higher order thinking to help students communicate their knowledge on a particular topic or concept, with the ultimate goal of having them craft their own questions. If the Hitchhiker's Galaxy had access to the learning frameworks and research based pedagogy to better frame the initial question of "What is the meaning of life, the universe, and everything?" how would the question have changed? And more importantly, how would it have changed the answer?

The Coast.Net shares that "in ASCII language, the most basic computer software, '42' is the designation for an asterisk. So, when Deep Thought was asked what the true meaning of life was, it answered as you might think a computer would - 42, in other words, "Anything you want it to be!" Which brings me to the Hitchhiker's Guide for Educators: The Canva Classroom. I want to share my process of starting with a standard and formulating good questions in order to design meaningful tasks.

Hopefully, if we scaffold students successfully then it won't take ten million years for deep thought (in reference to The Hitchhiker's Guide to the Galaxy's computer) to not only answer questions, but formulate their own! Now…how can Canva aid us in this task? Now that's a good question!

My Canva Introduction

I have been designing graphics, project based learning templates, presentations, and marketing materials myself for years (former Piktochart user), but I recently discovered Canva and the possibilities of what I could create expanded exponentially. My design universe became infinite in potential. I slowly graduated from using Canva for only social media to using it for everything! Instead of creating my presentations in Google Slides, Powerpoint, or Keynote, I started creating everything in the Canva platform. But I was still downloading PNG or JPEG files and uploading them as the background for my Google Drive presentations. Whether it was workshop presentations, keynotes, student notebooks, vocabulary activities, or any form of student assignments—I gravitated back to Canva, until eventually I ditched Google and other platforms all together. Especially, with the emergence of the Canva for Education platform.

Prior to my Canva discovery I was using bgremover.io to remove backgrounds from images, qrcodegenerator.com to create QR codes to share my work, the thenounproject.com for graphics, and many other standalone tools for projects. I quickly learned that I could replace all of those things with Canva. It is seriously the one platform to rule them all!

If Gollum was a designer, teacher, or entrepreneur this would totally be his precious! It has a background remover tool, a qr code generator, and a reservoir of photos, graphics, videos, and even templates, so you don't have to recreate the wheel, AND they are adding more everyday! But wait! There's more!

The final push for me to use Canva almost exclusively in my classroom outside of my LMS was the debut of Canva for Education. This was icing on the already pretty awesome cake. With Canva for Education, I was now able to create a Canva Classroom, which means anything I create in Canva I can send to students to edit collaboratively, or as a template to copy and work on individual assignments and projects. It even has a 'share with teacher' tool that enables students to share their work with me to review inside of the platform. I still post the links in my LMS (learning management system) as an assignment, but I can even do that from Canva as it pushes out assignments to Google Classroom, Microsoft Teams, Schoology, Canvas, and many more. If you are still not convinced, let me share an anecdote of success involving one of my students.

CREATIVITY UNLEASHED

In 2020, I was teaching 7th grade literature at a 1:1 private school in Louisville, Kentucky. The first student assignment I created and shared in Canva was simple—it was a digitized version of a one pager on our Gothic Literature unit. Students had to create a poster that used icons and images to communicate motif, characterization, setting, symbolism, and mood, while adding a thesis statement that communicated the theme. After their designs were submitted, I printed out their work and they had to find quotes that supported each of these elements.

Student engagement was through the roof and I had a 100% turn in rate. Previously, students would have to draw these by hand, and I got the push back of, "But Mrs. Fox, I'm not an artist." With Canva they were able to use the reservoir of millions of icons, graphics, texts, and photos to create an original work they could be proud of. One of my students told me that he didn't think of himself as creative, but with Canva it was hard not to do a good job and he was very proud of his work. That he couldn't wait until the next assignment!

This same student went on to join my Esports team and created logos, twitch channel headers, flyers for events at the school, and even backgrounds for the school musical. Introducing him to Canva as a new tool of design and communication unlocked the creativity inside of him that he didn't know was there. And that is what makes teaching so worth it.

> **Tools like Canva eliminate what students view as artistic barriers. It gives them a voice. It gives them the power of self-expression. You really can do anything with Canva.**

As an educator I strive to help students find ways to unlock their hidden potential. To help them become more, and realize that in the wise words of TheTechRabbi Michael Cohen, that "creativity is a mindset, not an art set." Tools like Canva eliminate what students view as artistic barriers. It gives them a voice. It gives them the power of self-expression. You really can do anything with Canva. Before we begin down the Canva rabbit hole, let's look at foundational frameworks that work in tandem with Canva as an instructional design tool.

FIGHT YOUR WAY *Through*

"NOBODY TELLS THIS TO PEOPLE WHO ARE BEGINNERS. I WISH SOMEONE TOLD ME. ALL OF US WHO DO CREATIVE WORK, WE GET INTO IT BECAUSE WE HAVE GOOD TASTE. BUT THERE IS THIS GAP.

FOR THE FIRST COUPLE YEARS YOU MAKE STUFF, IT'S JUST NOT THAT GOOD. IT'S TRYING TO BE GOOD, IT HAS POTENTIAL, BUT IT'S NOT. BUT YOUR TASTE, THE THING THAT GOT YOU INTO THE GAME, IS STILL KILLER. AND YOUR TASTE IS WHY YOUR WORK DISAPPOINTS YOU.

A LOT OF PEOPLE NEVER GET PAST THIS PHASE. THEY QUIT. MOST PEOPLE I KNOW WHO DO INTERESTING, CREATIVE WORK WENT THROUGH YEARS OF THIS. WE KNOW OUR WORK DOESN'T HAVE THIS SPECIAL THING THAT WE WANT IT TO HAVE.

WE ALL GO THROUGH THIS. AND IF YOU ARE JUST STARTING OUT OR YOU ARE STILL IN THIS PHASE, YOU GOTTA KNOW ITS NORMAL AND THE MOST IMPORTANT THING YOU CAN DO IS DO A LOT OF WORK.

PUT YOURSELF ON A DEADLINE SO THAT EVERY WEEK YOU WILL FINISH ONE STORY. IT IS ONLY BY GOING THROUGH A VOLUME OF WORK THAT YOU WILL CLOSE THAT GAP, AND YOUR WORK WILL BE AS GOOD AS YOUR AMBITIONS.

AND I TOOK LONGER TO FIGURE OUT HOW TO DO THIS THAN ANYONE I'VE EVER MET. IT'S GONNA TAKE AWHILE. IT'S NORMAL TO TAKE AWHILE. YOU'VE JUST GOTTA FIGHT YOUR WAY THROUGH."

— Ira Glass

3

DEPTH OF KNOWLEDGE

When I begin to plan my lessons for the week, I start by looking at what the standards are asking the students to know. Next, I think about what learning experiences I can create to ensure that students are engaging with the content in meaningful ways, and they are able to communicate their understanding. Depth of Knowledge is one of the frameworks I take into consideration when approaching any of my Canva designs.

I was recently in a professional learning community (PLC) meeting at my school and the topic of discussion was Norman Webb's Depth of Knowledge framework. Webb's DOK Levels essentially provides a framework that helps teachers understand the cognitive demand of standards and the depth and extent students must understand and use their learning (Refer to the chart on this page to get an overview of each level). In this PLC session, we discussed rigor to the point of ad nauseam mostly because there was a disconnect in our group's definition of what rigor is and which DOK level our standards-driven essential questions would fall. I think the confusion was introduced with the DOK Wheel.

If you are familiar with DOK, you have probably received the wheel as a guide in your training just like me! It sounded good right? The DOK Wheel is essentially a graphic that divides the four DOK Levels into segments – or more specifically, spokes. Within each spoke are cognitive action verbs that are supposed to designate a specific level of depth of knowledge. (Refer to the diagram-Wheel of DOK).

Unbeknownst to me at the time, the DOK Wheel has received educational scrutiny for suggesting the level of Depth of Knowledge demanded depends upon the cognitive action verb that indicates the type of thinking students must perform. Also, even though Norman Webb is cited on the DOK Wheel poster, he did not create the DOK Wheel and discourages its use. In an interview with John Walkup (2013) Webb said, "The only possible use of the chart I can see is if someone took a verb and asked how it could be placed in each of the four sectors." A training guide created by Mississippi educators also claims that "The objective's central verb(s) alone is/are not sufficient information to assign a DOK level." Developers must also consider the complexity of the task and/or information, conventional levels of prior knowledge for students at the grade level, and the mental processes used to satisfy the requirements set forth in the objective. Furthermore, John Walkup, PhD goes on to explain how the wheel is misleading.

"As one example, the action verb design appears in the DOK-4 section of the wheel chart. However, a teacher asking students to design an engineering apparatus is not assigning a DOK-4 level activity unless she prompts her students to employ mathematical or scientific principles into their design. And although the verb "calculate" appears in the DOK-1 section of the wheel chart, I can assure the reader that many mathematical calculations can reach up far into DOK-4."

Which leaves me with the question: How do we know what level of DOK the standards are asking, and what tasks can we create to ensure we are helping students not just meet, but exceed that expectation?

I know from my research that not all assignments and tasks need to fall into the level four category, and that it's normal to have a variety of tasks of different rigor. I also understand that a student doesn't need to master a task in category one to be successful at a category 4 task.

But—I'm still not an expert on this topic, so I have brought in Erik Francis, author of Deconstructing Depth of Knowledge: A Method and Model for Deeper Teaching and Learning and Now That's A Good Question! to guide us through the depths of DOK. Let's start by going back to the essentials of lesson designs, starting with asking good questions. Before we get into Erik's guest piece, take a look at his graphic on DOK.

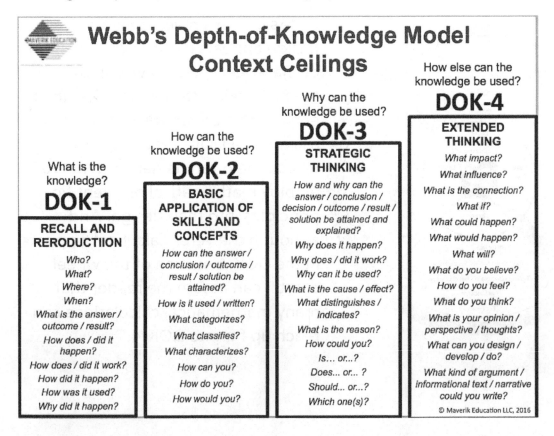

GUEST PIECE BY ERIK FRANCIS
EXPLAINING DOK

For the last ten years, Depth of Knowledge has been a focus and priority in education. Unfortunately, much of the information that's been presented and provided about DOK has been inaccurate and inconsistent. This is due to inaccurate visuals such as the DOK Wheel. These graphics have given educators the wrong impression and interpretation of Depth of Knowledge as a concept and a framework.

Depth of Knowledge and the DOK Levels are not another way to "do Bloom's", which is how it's commonly (and incorrectly) considered and explained. Depth of Knowledge is not based on the complexity of thinking students must demonstrate as indicated by the verb. The DOK Levels are not a taxonomy that classifies the complexity of cognitive processes or scaffolds upon each other. Both Depth of Knowledge and the DOK Levels should also not be used to critique the complexity or quality of a teaching and learning experience.

So what exactly is Depth of Knowledge and how can the DOK Levels be used to plan and provide rigorous teaching and learning experiences?

DEPTH OF KNOWLEDGE AS AN ACADEMIC CONCEPT

Depth of Knowledge is a different and deeper way of looking at the goals and expectations of academic standards, curricular activities, and assessment items. It demands us to look beyond the verb to clarify the complexity of the content students will learn and confirm the context in which students must understand and use their learning. That's all described and detailed by the words and phrases that follow the initial cognitive action verb of a learning intention, objective, or target. For example:

"Compare and contrast stories in the same genre (e.g., mysteries and adventure stories) on their approaches to similar themes and topics." (ELA-LITERACY-5.9)

The learning intention of this English language arts standard features two cognitive action verbs: "to compare" and "to contrast". These are the types of thinking the standard expects students to demonstrate. Traditionally, we would judge the complexity (and even the quality) of an academic standard, curricular activity, or assessment item based on the verb and where it's listed in a learning taxonomy such as Bloom's Revised Taxonomy. However, what exactly does the standard demand students to compare and contrast? Also, how deeply does the standard demand students to compare and contrast?

That's what Depth of Knowledge considers. To determine the level of Depth of Knowledge demanded, we need to clarify and confirm the following:

- <u>What exactly must students learn</u>? This is identified by the noun or noun phrase that names the key concept or content students must think about or study. It's usually the first noun or noun phrase that immediately follows the initial cognitive action verb of a learning intention, objective, or target.

For example, in this ELA standard, the noun "stories" identifies what students must compare and contrast. That's also the noun that describes the performance expectation of the standard.

- <u>How deeply must students understand and use their learning?</u> That's informed by all the words and phrases that follow the initial cognitive action verb of a learning intention, objective, or target. Those words and phrases detail the conditions and criteria – or context – for students to understand and use their knowledge and thinking. For example, this ELA standard demands that students must not only compare but also contrast. The verb "to compare" is the primary cognitive action students must perform. However, the cognitive action verb "to contrast" is part of the conditions and criteria because it follows the initial cognitive action verb. It also informs that students must perform more than one cognitive action or step to achieve the standard. The plural noun "stories" informs how many texts students must compare and contrast. The rest of the words and phrases that complete the statement of objective details the conditions (i.e., "in the same genre") and criteria [i.e., "(e.g., mysteries and adventure stories) on their approaches to similar themes and topics"] of the performance expectation.

Essentially, determining the Depth of Knowledge demanded involves going further with unpacking or unwrapping the standards. After we circle the verbs and underline the nouns that indicate the knowledge and skills students must develop and demonstrate, we must look closely at all the words and phrases that follow that initial cognitive action verb to clarify what exactly and confirm how deeply students must understand and use their knowledge and thinking – or learning. That will determine and designate the level of Depth of Knowledge demanded.

DEPTH OF KNOWLEDGE AS AN ACADEMIC FRAMEWORK

The DOK Levels can be used as a method and model for developing and delivering teaching and learning experiences that will demand students to understand and use their learning in different contexts. Each DOK level has a specific instructional focus and addresses a unique overarching essential question.

DOK-1: What is the knowledge or skill?
DOK 1 teaching and learning experiences focus on Knowledge Acquisition. Students must acquire and develop the foundational knowledge and functional understanding they need to succeed in a subject area. Activities, items, and tasks require students to recall information or recall how to "just do it" to answer questions, solve problems, complete tasks, or read and respond to texts and topics correctly.

LET'S MAKE A DOK 1!

The goals and expectations of a DOK 1 teaching and learning experience are similar to a quiz show such as Jeopardy! and Who Wants to Be a Millionaire? These TV shows only require contestants to recall "just the facts" or recall how to "just do it" to answer correctly. Plus, think about how the questions are phrased on these shows. On Jeopardy!, the host presents a cue or a clue and the contestants respond with a question that asks who, where, where, or when. On Who Wants to Be a Millionaire?, the contestants are presented with multiple choice questions that have only one answer. The activities, items, and tasks in a DOK 1 teaching and learning experiences will resemble the questions asked on these shows. However, you can make this an active, creative, and engaging experience for your students by modeling the teaching and learning experience after one of these quiz shows (e.g., present information and have students respond in the form of a question; allow them to do a 50/50, poll the audience / class, have a classmate or friend in another class be a lifeline).

DOK 1 CANVA CONNECTION:

The quiz show templates within Canva can be used to plan and provide active and engaging DOK 1 teaching and learning experiences that resemble a quiz show. Canva also features quiz show templates that resemble Computer-Adaptive Test (CAT) items featured on digitized state summative and site-based benchmark assessments. You can also create or import templates into Canva that resemble the graphics used on game shows (e.g., the Jeopardy! choice board, the scaffolded multiple choice scale that shows progression, or visuals featuring the multiple choice question).

"THE SIMPLEST WAY TO DEEPEN A TEACHING AND LEARNING EXPERIENCE FROM A DOK 1 TO A DOK 2 IS TO CHALLENGE THE STUDENTS TO EXPLAIN HOW AND WHY THEY UNDERSTAND OR CAN USE WHAT THEY HAVE LEARNED TO ATTAIN A SPECIFIC RESPONSE OR RESULT. "

<u>DOK-2: How and why can knowledge and skills be used?</u>
A DOK 2 teaching and learning experience addresses and assesses <u>Knowledge Application</u>. Students must establish and explain with examples how and why they can apply knowledge, concepts, and skills or use information and basic reasoning to answer questions, address problems, accomplish tasks, or analyze the ideas and information presented in texts or pertaining to topics. The examples can be the items (e.g. math problems) or information (data and facts) presented in a text.

DOK 2 activities, items, and tasks also require students to answer correctly. However, unlike DOK 1 teaching and learning experiences, which focuses on rote learning and responses, a DOK 2 teaching and learning experience demands students to develop and demonstrate conceptual and procedural understanding. The simplest way to deepen a teaching and learning experience from a DOK 1 to a DOK 2 is to challenge the students to explain how and why they understand or can use what they have learned to attain a specific response or result.

DOK 2 teaching and learning experiences promote social and emotional learning because they prompt students to consider and communicate their opinions, perspective, or thoughts. This is when students will be asked good effective questions such as "What do you believe?", "How do you feel?", or "What are your thoughts?" That's another key difference between DOK 1 and DOK 2 teaching and learning experience. Students progress from recalling and restating "just the facts" to expressing and sharing their feelings or reasoning.

LET'S MAKE A DOK 2!

In a DOK 2 teaching and learning experience, the spotlight shifts from the teacher to the student who must demonstrate and communicate how and why they understand and can use concepts and procedures. In essence, the student becomes the teacher or the "star of the show". They are like Bob Ross explaining how he can use his knowledge and skills in painting to paint landscapes, or Rachael Ray demonstrating and communicating how they can prepare meals in 30 minutes or less using the terminology of cooking. The teacher is like the director or producer of the show, presenting the objective and task, calling, "Action!" and having the student take charge of the teaching and learning.

DOK 2 CANVA CONNECTION:

You can use Canva's video and social media templates to have students produce their own "show" – or instructional video – where they demonstrate and communicate how they understand or can use what they have learned to answer questions, address problems, accomplish tasks, or analyze the ideas and information presented in texts or pertaining to topics. These videos can be transmitted as a private exchange between the student and their teacher. Students could also be encouraged to produce their own video series, social media page, or podcast where they can express and share their knowledge and skills not only in their own unique way, but also in a language or manner other students their age or grade level could understand.

DOK 3: How and why could the knowledge and skills be used?

DOK 3 teaching and learning experience engage students in <u>Knowledge Analysis</u>. Students are engaged to think strategically or use complex reasoning supported by evidence to examine and explain actions, answers, or arguments – be their own or those made by others. That's the key shift between a DOK 2 to a DOK 3 teaching and learning experience. Students move from comprehending and communicating their learning like a teacher to thinking like a disciplinarian (e.g., a mathematician, a scientist, a literary or arts critic, a historian, an artist or musician, an athletic team captain or coach). They progress from attaining and explaining answers to justifying or refuting responses, results, or reasoning. They also shift from expressing and sharing emotions and examples to crafting and critiquing arguments with evidentiary support.

One way to engage students in a DOK 3 teaching and learning experience is to present students with an answer – or multiple answers – and engage them to defend, justify, or refute with evidence which is (or are) accurate or appropriate given the conditions or criteria. Another way to engage students in a DOK 3 teaching and learning experience is to present students with a scenario or situation, change the conditions or criteria, and have students think critically or creatively what the outcome, result, or solution could be given the change in circumstances.

LET'S MAKE A DOK 3!

A DOK 3 teaching and learning experience resembles two different formats of television shows. It could resemble a skills-based reality competition such as Top Chef! or LegoMasters, which engages participants to think strategically how and why they could use their knowledge and skills to complete a specific task within a set timeframe. DOK 3 teaching and learning experiences also resemble TV guest panels, or talk shows such as news shows on CNN or FOX or sports shows on ESPN for FOX Sports. These shows are moderated by a facilitator who engages in debates and dialogues about a complex topic.

DOK 3 CANVA CONNECTION:

DOK 3 Canva connections involves activity templates in Canva that engage students in active strategy or skills-based learning experiences. For example using hexagonal thinking to have students make connections between terms and concepts while defending their answers. They can also use the video templates to produce video panels or talk shows similar to the news and sports shows they watch on broadcast or cable television, compare and contrast two pieces of literature with textual evidence, examine multiple solutions methods for math problems, examining an author's purpose of a text and using evidence to support their claims, or comparing and contrasting the life cycles of frogs versus butterflies.

DOK 4: What else could be done with the knowledge?
DOK 4 teaching and learning experiences encourage Knowledge Augmentation. Students are prompted to think extensively or explore and explain with examples and evidence how and why they could understand and use what they have learned deep within a subject area, among texts and topics, across the curriculum, or beyond the classroom.

DOK 4 teaching and learning experiences usually take an extended amount of time to complete. However, time is a characteristic of a DOK 4 teaching and learning experience, not a criterion. They are also not necessarily always project-based. What distinguishes a DOK 4 from all the other levels is their authenticity. Students are encouraged to develop their education, experience, and endowments (e,g. Innate gifts and skills) into personal expertise they could use to address, explain, or respond to a real world scenario or situation. DOK 4 teaching and learning experiences also demonstrate and communicate their expertise by speaking in-depth, innovatively, insightfully, and in their own unique way about a text or topic.

Examples of DOK 4 teaching and learning experiences are author or genre studies; STEM, STEAM, or STREAM learning experiences that address, explain, or respond to a real world scenario or situation; capstone projects; or expeditionary and service learning experiences.

LET'S MAKE A DOK 4!

DOK 4 teaching and learning experiences resemble the intricate and involved scenarios and situations students will experience in life professionally and personally. These scenarios and situations are showcased on reality TV business shows that have individuals with specific expertise and think extensively how they could address a wicked problem. For example, on Kitchen Nightmares, chef Gordon Ramsay is tasked to use his expertise in the culinary arts and restaurant management to turn around an eatery that's struggling or unsuccessful due to uncontrollable and unpredictable circumstances. DOK 4 teaching and learning experiences can also resemble shows like Shark Tank where entrepreneurs, innovators, and inventors pitch their project to a panel of investors who decide whether their plan or product is worth funding.

DOK 4 CANVA CONNECTION:

For DOK 4, students can use Canva to create video pitches, they can create a business and build a company website using Canva's website builder, or use presentation templates to have students communicate solutions to design challenges or genius hour presentations. Amanda uses a great example of Sustainable Development Goals and solving world problems in the template section of this book.

DOK 1	DOK 2	DOK 3	DOK 4
What is the knowledge?	How can the knowledge be applied?	How can the knowledge solve problems?	How can the knowledge be extended?

Recall and Rote Response	Applied Concepts and Skills	Strategic Thinking	Extended Thinking

When planning and providing teaching and learning for Depth of Knowledge using the DOK Levels, always use these questions to guide how you develop and deliver the experience:

- What are the words and phrases that follow the cognitive action verb?
- What exactly is the content knowledge (subject or skill) must students learn?
- How deeply must students understand and use their learning?
- What is the instructional focus and purpose of the DOK teaching and learning experience?
- What is the overarching question the DOK teaching and learning experience addresses?
- How could the Canva templates be used to address and assess student learning at the DOK Level demanded by the academic standard, curricular activity, or assessment item?

Erik Francis, author of Now That's a Good Question! addresses formulating good questions modifying Norman Webb's Depth of Knowledge Wheel, while also taking into consideration Casel's 5 SEL competencies and Carol Dweck's concept of Growth Mindset and Bloom's Taxonomy.

ASKING GOOD QUESTIONING IN MY OWN WORK

The foundation of a good Canva template is dependent on how it asks students to engage with the content, and what mental complexity is involved in the task. The most recent design challenge came to me out of curiosity in the form of this question: "Can I use Canva to create a book on how to use Canva?" If I were asking my students this, it would be a simple yes or no question. Yes. You can. Or maybe some would say no, or I don't know enough about the platform to answer this question. Regardless, there was little rigor or actionable verbiage. The next question was "How can I use Canva to create a book on how to use Canva in the classroom?" This question drove me down a rabbit hole of inquiry. This question launched a million more questions.

- Do I want to print my book?
- If so, what format do I need to design it in?
- What size does the book need to be?
- What is a bleed? Can I set up print bleeds in Canva?
- What format do I need to export my book in?
- Where can I have my book printed?
- How can I sell and distribute it?

Once I figured out the technical aspects of Canva, my questions shifted to a more content based focus.

- What do teachers need to know about Canva?
- How do I convey the power Canva has in the classroom?
- How can I help other teachers manage their workflow?
- Which Canva features will I showcase?
- What templates can I design that will be most beneficial to teachers?
- How can I share the connection between DOK, questioning, and designing tasks?

On the next three pages I have compiled graphics to help you ask the right questions prior to creating a template or activity, understand DOK levels and activities that align with each level, and also examples of templates you can replicate and apply in your own practice.

CREATED BY @AMANDAFOXSTEM

DEPTH OF KNOWLEDGE
+ Canva CONNECTIONS
PLANNING GUIDE

LEVEL 1

RECALL AND REPRODUCE

LEVEL 2

APPLY KNOWLEDGE OF SKILLS AND CONCEPTS

LEVEL 3

STRATEGIC THINKING

LEVEL 4

EXTENDED THINKING

#THE Canva CLASSROOM

CREATED BY @AMANDAFOXSTEM BASED ON THE WORK OF ERIK FRANCIS

DEPTH OF KNOWLEDGE
+ Canva GOOD QUESTIONS

any Questions?

LEVEL 1

- WHO?
- WHAT?
- WHERE?
- WHEN?
- HOW?
- WHY?

LEVEL 2

- HOW DOES IT HAPPEN?
- HOW DOES IT WORK?
- HOW IS IT USED?
- WHAY IS THE ANSWER?
- WHAT IS THE OUTCOME?
- WHAT IS THE RESULT?
- WHAT CAN YOU DO?
- HOW CAN YOU USE IT?
- HOW WOULD YOU USE IT?

LEVEL 3

- WHY DOES IT WORK?
- WHY IS THE ANSWER?
- WHY IS THE OUTCOME?
- WHY IS THE RESULT?
- WHAT DOES IT INFER?
- WHAT DOES IT SUGGEST?
- WHAT IS THE CAUSE/EFFECT?
- WHAT DISTINGUISHES/INDICATES?
- WHAT IS THE REASON?
- WHAT IS THE RELATIONSHIP?
- HOW COULD YOU DEVELOP AND USE A MODEL?
- HOW COULD YOU?

LEVEL 4

- WHAT IS THE IMPACT?
- WHAT IS THE INFLUENCE?
- WHAT IF?
- WHAT WOULD HAPPEN?
- WHAT COULD HAPPEN?
- WHAT WILL?
- WHAT ELSE?
- HOW ELSE?
- WHAT DO YOU BELIEVE, THINK, FEEL?
- WHAT CAN YOU BUILD/CREATE/DESIGN/DEVELOP/PRODUCE?
- WHAT KIND OF A PLAN COULD YOU DEVELOP?
- WHAT KIND OF TEXT COULD YOU WRITE?
- WHAT KIND OF PROBLEM COULD YOU PRESENT?

SOURCE: FRAMEWORK ADAPTED FROM WEBB, 1997,2002; HESS 2009A, 2009B

#THE Canva CLASSROOM

DEPTH OF KNOWLEDGE

+ Canva TEMPLATES

LEVEL 1

CANVA JEOPARDY

THIS TEMPLATE PROMPTS STUDENTS TO RECALL INFORMATION THROUGH A TRIVIA GAME.

LEVEL 2

IRON CHEF

IN A DOK 2 TEACHING AND LEARNING EXPERIENCE, THE SPOTLIGHT SHIFTS FROM THE TEACHER TO THE STUDENT. THE TEACHER IS LIKE THE DIRECTOR OR PRODUCER OF THE SHOW, PRESENTING THE OBJECTIVE AND TASK, CALLING, "ACTION!" AND HAVING THE STUDENT TAKE CHARGE OF THE TEACHING AND LEARNING.

LEVEL 3

LEGO MASTERS

A DOK 3 TEACHING AND LEARNING EXPERIENCE RESEMBLES TWO DIFFERENT FORMATS OF TELEVISION SHOWS. IT COULD RESEMBLE A SKILLS-BASED REALITY COMPETITION SUCH AS TOP CHEF! OR LEGOMASTERS THAT ENGAGES PARTICIPANTS TO THINK STRATEGICALLY HOW AND WHY THEY COULD USE THEIR KNOWLEDGE AND SKILLS TO COMPLETE A SPECIFIC TASK WITHIN A SET TIMEFRAME.

LEVEL 4

SHARK TANK

DOK 4 TEACHING AND LEARNING EXPERIENCES RESEMBLE THE INTRICATE AND INVOLVED SCENARIOS AND SITUATIONS STUDENTS WILL EXPERIENCE IN LIFE PROFESSIONALLY AND PERSONALLY. THESE SCENARIOS AND SITUATIONS ARE SHOWCASED ON REALITY TV BUSINESS SHOWS THAT HAVE INDIVIDUALS WITH SPECIFIC EXPERTISE THINK EXTENSIVELY HOW THEY COULD ADDRESS A WICKED PROBLEM.

#THE Canva CLASSROOM

4

DESIGNING FOR LEARNING

I am currently a member of numerous writing groups, and we often talk about if we are planners or pantsers when we approach writing. Before sitting down to write, a planner spends time constructing story elements. A pantser starts writing without having a clear direction or plan.

When it comes to writing, I determine what I want readers to get out of my story, make a plot outline, flesh out my characters, and then plot out the events that will lead my characters to their destination. I am a planner. To get to a climactic point and resolution, I work backwards to develop my story. This got me thinking about my approach to education and teaching. Am I a planner…or a pantser?

When it comes to education, there are occasions when… I hate to admit it, but I have been a pantser. I mean, there are only so many hours in a day, and it seems like I teach a different subject every year. Instead of creating a solid plan, I would fly by the seat of my pants and try new tools or activities with my students on the spur of the moment.

To be honest, even in the sphere of teaching, being a pantser necessitates some level of planning. When I first started teaching a decade ago, I had no idea where to begin when it came to creating a learning exercise for kids. The expectations of having a plan for everything were anxiety-inducing as well. It was easier to be more short-sighted and pants it.

Also, being a fresh out of college educator and a total tech nerd, I would often jump on the bandwagon of whatever new tool crossed my path. Augmented reality! Awesome! Let's get started! Powtoon! Oh! I want my students to make awesome animated videos! With technology adoption, I was all over the place. Either the technology or the activity drove the learning experience rather than the learning goals. They dictated how I taught, chose tools, and assessed the content.

Oftentimes, I would revisit the activities that students had taken part in and then design an evaluation that matched the path we had taken to get to where we were. This process is considered a "forward design" approach where teachers envision how they will teach content, create an activity, and then attempt to later connect it to standards and learning goals or design an evaluation tool. This method of instruction does not necessarily produce transferrable learning.

As we approach designing activities and assessments in Canva, I want to make sure that you have a good approach to designing activities and don't make the same mistake I did; instead, put learning outcomes and cognitive rigor in the driver seat by having a well laid out plan! I'll go over the basics of the Understanding by Design Framework to planning in the next part, with examples of how to use Canva in tandem with a strategy rather than just for the sake of the tool.

UNDERSTANDING BY DESIGN

Wiggins and McTighe (2017), authors of Understanding by Design, state that "Our lessons, units, and courses should be logically inferred from the results sought, not derived from the methods, books, and activities with which we are most comfortable," through what they call a 'Backwards Design' approach. "Backwards design is less of a philosophy or approach to teaching, but a planning framework," to intentionally design in a more goal-focused fashion (Wiggins, 2014).

Backwards Design, like Webb's Depth of Knowledge, starts with standards and asks what students need to be able to do as a result of that standard, along with the purpose of the activities to measure student learning. If we examine and utilize both of these frameworks, we can be sure we're building lessons and courses that both challenge students and put learning outcomes at the forefront of the instructional design.

Identify desired results.

Determine acceptable evidence.

Plan learning experiences and instruction.

We are also developing a blueprint for the lesson or course that we are going to teach when we deconstruct standards and generate driving questions or essential questions for students. These questions will serve as a springboard for the instruction and assessments we will create, with the goal of ensuring that learning is the primary focus. Remember the age-old adage, tasks before apps? Prior to creating the tasks, we must think about the learning outcomes and create tasks that will help students achieve them. This also prevents students from participating in time-consuming or superficial tasks that aren't indicative of actual learning or cognitive rigor. An excellent activity places the student at the center of the learning process, leaving the teacher to guide them from the sidelines.

There are also short-term and long-term goals to consider. Short-term goals may resemble comprehension checks and knowledge building. Formative assessments are an excellent indicator of this. Long-term goals acquaint themselves with unit plans and require skill-building or synthesis of information and can take on the form of culminating projects or term papers. Both are required for effective planning.

While Canva is the tool of focus, this section is designed to shift attention away from the platform and onto the learning that occurs and what students can convey or demonstrate using it. Because the tool is content-agnostic and has a variety of ways teachers can design instructional content as well as assess students, it's easier for it to become a vehicle for not only teacher-created content, but also student created designs.

A good design combines information and performance while also utilizing critical and creative thinking. Canva fosters student creation as evidence of long-term goals through projects, which is one of its strengths. While tests can promote critical thinking, for the purpose of this book, student-designed artifacts created on the Canva platform will serve as the primary evidence of student mastery.

CREATED BY @AMANDAFOXSTEM

BACKWARDS DESIGN
+ Canva

THIS GRAPHIC WAS INFORMED BY THE WORK OF WIGGINS AND MCTIGHE'S THREE STEPS TO BACKWARDS DESIGN TO HELP ENSURE YOU ARE PLANNING APPROPRIATE ACTIVITIES WITH IDEAS FOR EVALUATIONS AND INSTRUCTIONAL STRATEGIES YOU CAN CREATE WITH CANVA.

1 IDENTIFY DESIRED RESULTS

STARTING WITH THE STANDARDS. CREATE ESSENTIAL QUESTIONS TO PROMOTE COGNITIVE ENGAGEMENT AND ANSWER THE FOLLOWING QUESTIONS.

- WHAT INFORMATION DO I NEED TO PROVIDE TO STUDENTS?
- WHAT KNOWLEDGE AND SKILLS SHOULD STUDENTS MASTER?
- WHAT ARE THE BIG IDEAS OR ENDURING UNDERSTANDINGS?

2 DETERMINE ACCEPTABLE EVIDENCE

- WHAT TYPES OF LEARNING EXPERIENCES CAN WE DESIGN?
- WHAT IS ACCEPTABLE EVIDENCE, OR HOW WILL STUDENTS DEMONSTRATE THEIR KNOWLEDGE?

THIS IS THE PART WHERE YOU DEVELOP THE PERFORMANCE TASK OR ASSESSMENT TOOL. IN CANVA IT COULD BE ANY OF THE FOLLOWING:

- COLLABORATIVE PRESENTATION

- VIDEO PRESENTATION

 • A WIZER INTERACTIVE WORKSHEET

 • SCIENCE PROJECT

 • BOOK CREATOR PROJECT

 • SKETCHNOTES

• BROCHURES

 • INFOGRAPHICS

• WEBSITES

• STUDENT PORTFOLIOS

3 PLAN LEARNING EXPERIENCES

CONSIDERING THE LEARNING GOALS AND OUTCOMES, HOW WILL I TEACH TO ENSURE STUDENTS REACH THESE GOALS?

IN CANVA YOU CAN SEARCH LESSONS AND TEMPLATES CREATED BY TEACHERS, OR USE THE FOLLOWING INSTRUCTIONAL STRATEGIES TO CREATE YOUR OWN.

- GUIDED NOTES

- PEARDECK + CANVA INTERACTIVE LESSONS

 • HYPERDOCS: GUIDED INQUIRY

 • FLIPPED VIDEOS

 • CANVA.LIVE PRESENTATIONS

 • SCAVENGER HUNTS

 • BITMOJI CLASSROOMS

 • CORNELL NOTES

#THE Canva CLASSROOM

The graphic on the previous page lists ways you can use Canva in conjunction with UbD. While it is not exhaustive, it should serve as a starting point for developing instructional content and assessments in Canva. Skip forward to the chapter on Teaching with Canva and Canva Templates to learn more about these strategies!

LESSON PLANS

Lesson plans are one of those necessities of education that can often become a burden depending on administration and district requirements. I have been in multiple schools and districts in my decade of teaching, and every school has had a different requirement; from no lesson plans needed, to scripting out the entire class. With the latter, I felt I spent just as much time writing my plans as I did teaching!

While the Understanding by Design framework is a good planning approach, writing lesson plans with each of the elements present is cumbersome and time consuming. I have created several abbreviated templates that you can use to save time and become a more efficient planner. Check with your school and district requirements prior to using them!

The meat and potatoes of the framework are the standards, essential questions, student goals/tasks, instructional strategy and formative and summative assessment. On the next few pages I have included three templates you can use: A single lesson plan template, a weekly lesson plan template, and a daily agenda slide deck. The single lesson plan and weekly plan templates are more meant to be shared with administration, while the daily agenda can be shared with admin, parents, and students to communicate what is going on in your classroom each day. Hopefully, you are not in a district that requires all! The lesson plan format I use in the template section of the book is a little more detailed for the sake of replication and clarity of execution. In reality, lesson plan templates are a wheel meant to be remixed for your usability.

SINGLE LESSON PLANS

If you are writing a single lesson plan that you would like to share with other educators, I recommend using this template so it's easier for replication.

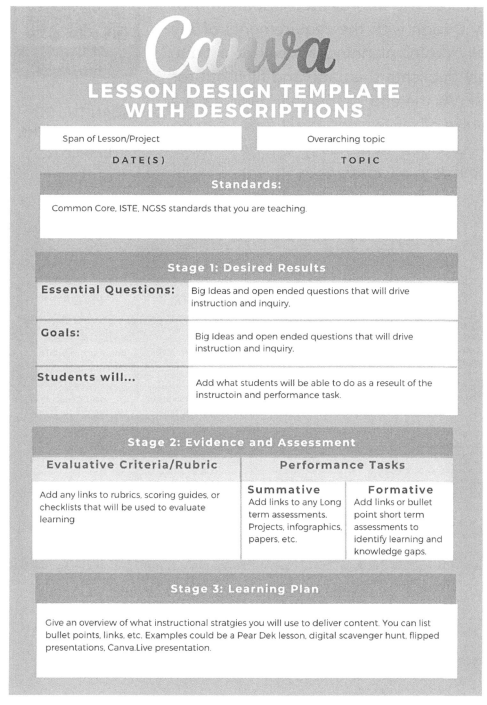

SCAN THE QR CODE TO GET THE TEMPLATE

WEEKLY LESSON PLANS

SCAN THE QR CODE TO GET THE TEMPLATE

These are required by the school district in which I currently teach. This is my abbreviated adaptation of Understanding by Design with the requirements of my school. I personally prefer planning a week at a time. Each week I simply duplicate the page and fill it out for the following week. At the end of the year, I will have a week to week archive of my lessons. Next year I can go back and make changes depending on new tools, strategies, and the kids in my classroom.

Weekly Lessons

DATES

MONDAY	TUESDAY	WEDNESDAY	THURSDAY	FRIDAY
Standards: Common Core, ISTE, NGSS,	Standards: Common Core, ISTE, NGSS,	Standards: Common Core, ISTE, NGSS,	Standards: Common Core, ISTE, NGSS,	Standards: Common Core, ISTE, NGSS,
Essential Questions: Big Ideas/Concepts in the from of questions.	Essential Questions: Big Ideas/Concepts in the from of questions.	Essential Questions: Big Ideas/Concepts in the from of questions.	Essential Questions: Big Ideas/Concepts in the from of questions.	Essential Questions: Big Ideas/Concepts in the from of questions.
Student Tasks: Students will....	Student Tasks: Students will....	Student Tasks: Students will....	Student Tasks: Students will....	Student Tasks: Students will....
Instructional Strategies: Teacher facilitated	Instructional Strategies: Teacher facilitated	Instructional Strategies: Teacher facilitated	Instructional Strategies: Teacher facilitated	Instructional Strategies: Teacher facilitated
Assessments: Evaluations/formative/ summative	Assessments: Evaluations/formative/ summative	Assessments: Evaluations/formative/ summative	Assessments: Evaluations/formative/ summative	Assessments: Evaluations/formative/ summative

Notes/Due Dates/ETC

Example of weekly lesson plan template.

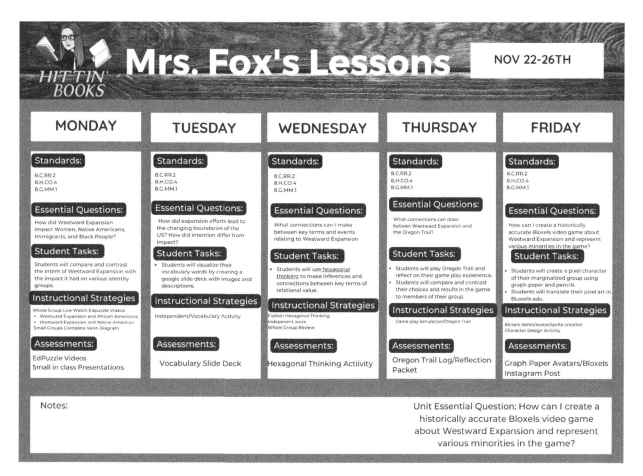

Example of populated weekly lesson plan template.

DAILY LESSON PLAN/AGENDA

Creating a daily agenda slide deck serves multiple purposes. It is written for the students, but can also serve as your lesson plans with administration. A lot of teachers use daily agendas to share learning goals and activities with families and students in addition to administrators. You typically find these projected at the beginning of class to communicate the day's expectations.

TODAY'S AGENDA: CANVA TEMPLATE REMIIXED

SCAN ME

EXAMPLE OF A MONTH OF LESSONS FOR STUDENTS FOR THE REMOTE/HYBRID CLASSROOM

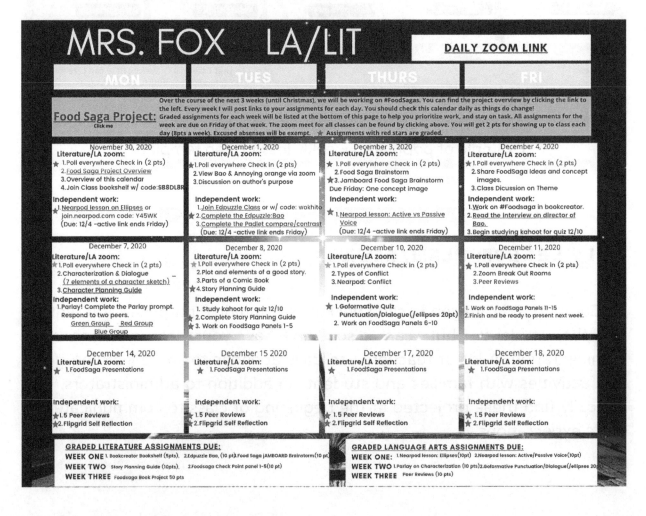

MRS. FOX   LA/LIT

DAILY ZOOM LINK

MON	TUES	THURS	FRI

Food Saga Project:
Click me

Over the course of the next 3 weeks (until Christmas), we will be working on #FoodSagas. You can find the project overview by clicking the link to the left. Every week I will post links to your assignments for each day. You should check this calendar daily as things do change! Graded assignments for each week will be listed at the bottom of this page to help you prioritize work, and stay on task. All assignments for the week are due on Friday of that week. The zoom meet for all classes can be found by clicking above. You will get 2 pts for showing up to class each day (8pts a week). Excused absenses will be exempt. ★ Assignments with red stars are graded.

November 30, 2020
Literature/LA zoom:
★ 1. Poll everywhere Check in (2 pts)
2. Food Saga Project Overview
3. Overview of this calendar
4. Join Class bookshelf w/ code:SB8DL8R

Independent work:
★ 1. Nearpod lesson on Ellipses or join.nearpod.com code: Y45WK
(Due: 12/4 –active link ends Friday)

December 1, 2020
Literature/LA zoom:
★ 1. Poll everywhere Check in (2 pts)
2. View Bao & Annoying orange via zoom
3. Discussion on author's purpose

Independent work:
1. Join Edpuzzle Class or w/ code: wokhito
★ 2. Complete the Edpuzzle:Bao
3. Complete the Padlet compare/contrast
(Due: 12/4 –active link ends Friday)

December 3, 2020
Literature/LA zoom:
★ 1. Poll everywhere Check in (2 pts)
2. Food Saga Brainstorm
★ 3. Jamboard Food Saga Brainstorm
Due Friday: One concept image

Independent work:
★ 1. Nearpod lesson: Active vs Passive Voice
(Due: 12/4 –active link ends Friday)

December 4, 2020
Literature/LA zoom:
★ 1. Poll everywhere Check in (2 pts)
2. Share FoodSaga Ideas and concept images.
3. Class Discussion on Theme

Independent work:
1. Work on #Foodsaga in bookcreator.
2. Read the interview on director of Bao.
3. Begin studying kahoot for quiz 12/10

December 7, 2020
Literature/LA zoom:
★ 1. Poll everywhere Check in (2 pts)
2. Characterization & Dialogue (7 elements of a character sketch)
3. Character Planning Guide

Independent work:
1. Parlay! Complete the Parlay prompt. Respond to two peers.
Green Group   Red Group
Blue Group

December 8, 2020
Literature/LA zoom:
★ 1. Poll everwhere Check in (2 pts)
2. Plot and elements of a good story.
3. Parts of a Comic Book
★ 4. Story Planning Guide

Independent work:
1. Study kahoot for quiz 12/10
★ 2. Complete Story Planning Guide
★ 3. Work on FoodSaga Panels 1-5

December 10, 2020
Literature/LA zoom:
★ 1. Poll everywhere Check in (2 pts)
2. Types of Conflict
3. Nearpod: Conflict

Independent work:
★ 1. Goformative Quiz Punctuation/Dialogue(/ellipses 20pt)
2. Work on FoodSaga Panels 6-10

December 11, 2020
Literature/LA zoom:
★ 1. Poll everywhere Check in (2 pts)
2. Zoom Break Out Rooms
3. Peer Reviews

Independent work:
1. Work on FoodSaga Panels 11-15
2. Finish and be ready to present next week.

December 14, 2020
Literature/LA zoom:
★ 1. FoodSaga Presentations

Independent work:
★ 1. 5 Peer Reviews
★ 2. Flipgrid Self Reflection

December 15 2020
Literature/LA zoom:
★ 1. FoodSaga Presentations

Independent work:
★ 1. 5 Peer Reviews
★ 2. Flipgrid Self Reflection

December 17, 2020
Literature/LA zoom:
★ 1. FoodSaga Presentations

Independent work:
★ 1. 5 Peer Reviews
★ 2. Flipgrid Self Reflection

December 18, 2020
Literature/LA zoom:
★ 1. FoodSaga Presentations

Independent work:
★ 1. 5 Peer Reviews
★ 2. Flipgrid Self Reflection

GRADED LITERATURE ASSIGNMENTS DUE:
WEEK ONE 1. Bookcreator Bookshelf (5pts), 2. Edpuzzle Bao, (10 pt). Food Saga jAMBOARD Brainstorm (10 pt)
WEEK TWO Story Planning Guide (10pts), 2. Foodsaga Check Point panel 1-5 (10 pt)
WEEK THREE Foodsaga Book Project 50 pts

GRADED LANGUAGE ARTS ASSIGNMENTS DUE:
WEEK ONE 1. Nearpod lesson: Ellipses(10pt) 2. Nearpod lesson: Active/Passive Voice(10pt)
WEEK TWO 1. Parlay on Characterization (10 pts) 2. Goformative Punctuation/Dialogue(/ellipses 20pt)
WEEK THREE Peer Reviews (10 pts)

PROTIP: CANVA 'TIDY UP' FEATURE. KEEPING YOUR DESIGN INGREDIENTS IN LINE IS EASY WITH CANVA'S TIDY UP FEATURE. SIMPLY SELECT THREE OR MORE ELEMENTS YOU WANT TO ALIGN, CLICK ON 'POSITION' IN THE TOP PANEL, AND FIND 'TIDY UP' IN THE DROP-DOWN MENU. YOUR ELEMENTS WILL FALL IN LINE AND MAKE YOUR DESIGN LOOK MUCH CLEANER.

DESIGN AESTHETICS

DESIGNING FOR AESTHETICS AND INCLUSIVITY

In an ever-increasing digital world, and with the rise of remote learning, students are frequently asked to communicate their learning through artifacts they have designed. Teachers are also content creators, having the responsibility of generating educational content and delivering it both online and in person. They must develop videos, slide decks, infographics, one-pagers, and posters, among other things.

We often assign presentations and projects to students while assuming they have a basic understanding of design principles, whereas, in reality, most students struggle with design. As a result, the presentations are cluttered, with several typefaces, writing over photos that is illegible, little to no contrast between content and background, a lack of balance, and designs that are inconsistent from beginning to end.

Design is a concept that is rarely taught outside of art, film, and multimedia classes, but it is one that should be discussed at the start of the year. Modeling good design concepts in our own lessons is one of the most effective methods to teach it. Teachers must understand not only the aesthetics of design, but also how to design for inclusivity to do it effectively.

In this section, I'll go over eight basic design principles that students and teachers can immediately apply in design creation, as well as a basic overview of the element of representation from the Universal Design for Learning Framework to help teachers create learning experiences that their students can connect with and ultimately be successful. There is a distinction to be made between designing for aesthetics and designing for educational purposes. Let's start with the eight main principles of aesthetic design.

EIGHT PRINCIPLES OF GOOD DESIGN

The eight design principles are a wonderful place to start for teachers and students who are just getting started with design. The eight principles are: balance, alignment, emphasis, proportion, movement, pattern, contrast, and unity. Each principle is broken down in the graphic on the next page.

By using this graphic as a guide, we can create aesthetic designs and presentations for teaching. The great thing about Canva is the robust repository of templates that are already well designed and customizable. I recommend utilizing these principles as a guide even when customizing a template! These principles will gradually polish our designer eyes and soon become second nature with experience and time.

DESIGN PRINCIPLES

BALANCE

It refers to the arrangements of the elements in a work of art to create a sense of visual equilibrium or stability. Balance can be asymmetrical, symmetrical, or radial. Ask students if their design would be balanced if it were a scale. They can use this metaphor to assess whether their slide would tip left or right based on the positioning of elements in the design.

PROPORTION

A scaling of options in relation to one another. It is about the relationship and size of one object to another.

EMPHASIS

It is concerned with the dominant feature or center of interest of a work of art. Artists use emphasis to draw their audience into the most important part of the composition.Is there a strong emphasis on major concepts, big ideas, and important information? The design should pull the viewer's eyes to key features through bold text, color, sizing, and other measures. This also enhances the brain's ability to organize and commit information to memory.

UNITY

Unity is the harmony of all visual elements in a composition. No single element takes over. A single design has unity, but this must also be considered in the slide design. Repetition of the same colors, elements, fonts, and layout in a presentation will give it unity and continuity. This design concept is contingent on all of the other principles coordinating.

ALIGNMENT

Alignment is the way objects or text line up along a path. Usually text will be left, right, or center aligned. Are all of the elements in the design lined up with one another?

PATTERN

It is repeated use of an element or a group of elements (motif) in a recurring and predictable arrangement called a sequence.

MOVEMENT

A directed path of optical movement. Movement is the path the viewer's eye takes through the work of art, often to focal areas. This can be controlled with placement and size. How should the viewer interact with the design? What should they see first?

CONTRAST

A juxtaposition that accentuates difference. It is the arrangement of opposite elements and effects in a work of art. Often, contrast directs the audience to a focal point. It also helps to emphasize, create variety, visual interest, and drama.

SCAN THE QR CODE TO WATCH THE
VIDEO ON DESIGN PRINCIPLES

Canva is an excellent resource for aspiring designers. There are a lot of wonderful infographics on the site that can be found by searching 'design principles,' which can be printed and put on display in the classroom to remind students to use these elements.

SCAN FOR BLOG ON DESIGN PRINCIPLES CREATED BY CANVA

Additionally, under the 'Learn' tab, there are courses, tutorials, blogs, and other resources to share. I personally love how the courses are broken into digestible chunks of 1–2-minute videos covering concepts and features. Searching their blogs is a great method for finding tips and ideas for designs; like the one you can find by scanning the QR code to the right. The video provides an in-depth look at twenty principles of design to help beginners hone in on their designer eye. For students, I recommend keeping it to the basic eight as not to overwhelm them while giving them a good starting point.

UNIVERSAL DESIGN FOR LEARNING FRAMEWORK FOR TEACHER CREATED CONTENT

Now that we have covered designing for aesthetics, let's talk about designing for inclusivity. When we are using design in our own instructional materials, it is important to consider elements from the Universal Design for Learning Framework created by CAST to ensure equitable learning experiences are created. With the purpose of generating materials that are inclusive of all learners, the guide "offers a set of concrete suggestions that can be applied to any discipline or domain to ensure that all learners can access and participate in meaningful, challenging learning opportunities" (CAST, 2018). This is particularly true in the case of digital, online, and remote learning. CAST has a fantastic guide for teachers that asks key questions when planning and designing digital learning experiences. A digital version of these questions can be viewed on the next page.

Key Questions to Consider When Planning Lessons

Think about how learners will engage with the lesson.

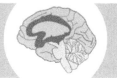

Does the lesson provide options that can help all learners:

- regulate their own learning?
- sustain effort and motivation?
- engage and interest all learners?

Think about how information is presented to learners.

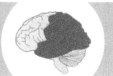

Does the information provide options that help all learners:

- reach higher levels of comprehension and understanding?
- understand the symbols and expressions?
- perceive what needs to be learned?

Think about how learners are expected to act strategically & express themselves.

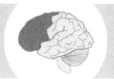

Does the activity provide options that help all learners:

- act strategically?
- express themselves fluently?
- physically respond?

From: *Universal Design for Learning: Theory and Practice*
Available at udltheorypractice.cast.org
For print and accessible EPUB, contact publishing@cast.org or any book retailer.

When creating designs, we should keep in mind that different learners process and perceive information in various ways. Some students may be blind, deaf, or have learning disabilities such as dyslexia or are English Language Learners that may require presenting information in multiple ways (CAST, 2018). When designing in Canva, it's important to keep these distinctions in mind. For example, using a dyslexia-friendly typeface in presentations or handouts might be an effective strategy to assist this student.

Including multiple representations of materials using a combination of audio, visual, and text can also help transfer information more easily as students may benefit more from one form of communication over another. Installing Microsoft's Immersive Reader add-on in Chrome is another alternative for having text read to students. There are extensions that work within Canva documents that you can use to eliminate the burden on the teacher to add audio to each design. While there is more to the UDL Framework than just representation, using the graphic on the next page to inform your design will help ensure you are designing for inclusivity.

In summary, knowing the students' strengths, weaknesses, and preferences will help inform the design approaches ensuring they are designed with every student in mind.

For a more comprehensive
look at the UDL Framework,
scan the QR code.

 # UNIVERSAL DESIGN FRAMEWORK + *Canva* TEMPLATES

THE UNIVERSAL DESIGN FOR LEARNING (UDL) IS A SET OF PRINCIPLES TO INFORM OUR DESIGNS. STATES THAT THE WAY WE DISPLAY INFORMATION IMPACTS HOW IT IS PERCEIVED. HERE ARE SEVEN TIPS TO CUSTOMIZE THE WAY WE DISPLAY INFORMATION.

CONTRAST BETWEEN BACKGROUND + TEXT

 **USE COLOR OR BOLD TEXT FOR EMPHASIS**

 **SPEED OR TIMING OF VIDEO, SOUND, ANIMATIONS**

 **THE LAYOUT OF VISUAL ELEMENTS**

CREATED BY @AMANDAFOXSTEM

 **VOLUME OR RATE OF SPEECH OR SOUND**

 **THE FONT USED FOR PRINT MATERIALS**

SIZE OF TEXT AND VISUAL ELEMENTS

SOURCE: CAST (2018). UNIVERSAL DESIGN FOR LEARNING GUIDELINES VERSION 2.2. RETRIEVED FROM HTTP://UDLGUIDELINES.CAST.ORG

#THE *Canva* CLASSROOM

TEACHING DESIGN PRINCIPLES TO STUDENTS

One of my favorite hooks to get students thinking about aesthetics is Corippo and Hebern's eduprotocol "The Worst Preso Ever." in this lesson, the youtube video 'Life After Death by Powerpoint," by comedian Don McMillan is shared. McMillan does an excellent and humorous job at covering what not to do when creating a presentation.

The Eduprotocol asks students to create a presentation breaking five principles of design. I like to partner that video with one that covers good design principles like "Principles of Design/Art," created by Kevin McMahon and Mike Horton on the Art Heroes channel. Students should be on their way to building an understanding of visual aesthetics. At the beginning of the year, I assign both videos to students through the Edpuzzle platform and then have them create "The Worst Preso Ever," in which they break the rules of design. Here is a Canva template that I created for the worst preso ever.

**WORST PRESO
EVER TEMPLATE**

TIPS FOR INTRODUCING STUDENTS TO DESIGN

1. Use and introduce students to the eight design principles when introducing Canva to students to get started with good designs from the start.
2. Consider UDL practices when designing materials to share information with students to ensure your lessons are inclusive of all students.
3. Start students off with Eduprotocol "The Worst Preso Ever" to drive home good design practices.
4. Model good design in your own presentations to reinforce these concepts.

Destination Two: Intro to Canva for Education

GETTING STARTED WITH Canva

Now that we explored asking good questions, creating tasks to drive inquiry and cognitive rigor, and principles of design, it is time to explore the Canva platform in all its glory! To reiterate, Canva is a powerful tool that students can utilize in their education and long after they are students in the classroom. When used effectively you can transform the way you teach and the way students learn and communicate. Equally important is being aware of joining a community of Canva using educators that are there to support and share resources and materials with you. We will go more in depth on joining these in the final destination of the book—the section on community and networking. To start, you can join my Facebook group 'The Canva Classroom" to start connecting and sharing with like-minded educators.

Before we go into the technical aspects of the platform and key features, let's review the 10 C's for the Canva Classroom. This graphic was made to be a guide to reflect on how we are using Canva and to remind us of not only what Canva has to offer, but also what we are bringing into the platform as teachers.

MADE IN *Canva*

10 C'S FOR THE CANVA CLASSROOM

CURRICULUM

Before creating a lesson, a task, assignment, or project, we need to come to the platform prepared. Knowing what standards we are teaching and what student expectations we hope to observe will help guide our design. Remember the principle of UDL? Start with an end in mind. If it is a lesson, what do you want the students to take away from it? If it is a task or project, what do you want to see reflected in student work?

CRITICAL THINKING

Analyze the tasks and templates that you are creating to ensure that students are challenged to extend their understanding of a topic, subject, or project. This starts with the curriculum, or standards, and design tasks that lead them down a path of inquiry. You can find some great templates that do this, but most will need to be altered to reflect the students in your classroom.

CANVAS

Canvas—Designing always starts with a canvas. There are plenty of templates you can choose from, or you can start with a blank canvas. When giving students an assignment, whether it is blank or a template, make sure that you have clearly communicated the learning goals and expectations so students successfully show what they have learned.

CREATIVITY

No matter who you are or what experience you have with design, there are plenty of features that help unlock creativity. Designs should be unique pieces and not a recipe. Templates are encouraged and can help those unfamiliar with the platform until they have played around with all Canva has to offer. The goal is to get students comfortable with customization.

CUSTOMIZATION

Try to customize and re-envision templates! Change the colors, fonts, and images to reflect your personality, but make sure that your designs are aesthetically pleasing. If you don't have a good eye for design yet, you can get there by paying attention to how templates look and mimic their layouts until you are comfortable to start from scratch!

CONFIDENCE

When it comes to Canva, the goal is to push students out of their comfort zones and embrace a growth mindset. Growth comes from discomfort, and while most will embrace the tool, some will be apprehensive or need help building confidence. You can differentiate skill sets by providing templates!

COLLABORATION

Canva is great for group work, collage boards, and group presentations! Working together is easy, interactive, and in real-time! Encourage group roles and have students set up these parameters in the beginning. There is also a document history/version, so if initially students accidentally erase someone else's work you can go back to a previous version!

COMMUNICATION

Canva allows students to not only share what they have learned in unique ways that honor their individuality, but it also allows them to share their work outside of the classroom. You can post links to projects, or download and upload work into other platforms, for example social media.

COMMUNITY

Outside of building a creative classroom community inside of the Canva Classroom, teachers and students can also share their work and ideas with the school, local, or global community.

CULTURE

Using Canva the nine ways above will certainly lead to a classroom culture that embraces individuality, student voice and choice, and also prepare them for college, careers, and life in the real world.

FIND THIS POSTER BY SCANNING THE QR CODE!

THE CANVA CLASSROOM OVERVIEW

THE CANVA PLATFORM IS COMPLETELY FREE!!

The first thing I want to mention is that Canva for Education is completely free. Educators and students have access to all of its features and utilities and there are a ton! In order to get a free account, you have to sign up with your teacher email, select that you are a teacher, and then verify your teacher status by providing a certificate or proof of employment. It may seem tedious, but it is so worth it!

FULL OF FREE READY-TO-USE TEMPLATES

One of the best features of Canva is that it comes equipped with ready-made templates; you can choose from thousands of ready-to-use educational templates for any subject, grade, or topic, and customize them to fit the needs of the students in your classroom. Inside of the platform you can create lessons and assignments that are as aesthetic as they are educational using copyright-free images, fonts, videos, animations, and editing features.

A TON OF FEEDBACK FUNCTIONS!

Whether you are in-person or virtual, you can share, review, and give feedback on their work in real-time or asynchronously. There is also a function to provide impactful feedback as students share their designs by commenting on student work and sending it back as either approved, or needs changes. You could also opt to add your own text or visual sticker comments. I like to do this with my Bitmoji character, as the platform has Bitmoji embedded directly into it! I will go over more app integrations Canva offers in the subsequent destination.

EASILY INTEGRATES WITH YOUR LMS!

Another convenient feature is it easily integrates with all most learning management platforms —Canvas, Schoology, D2L, Moodle, Blackboard, Google Classroom, and Microsoft Teams—making it easy to post and collect assignments in additional places that support the workflow you already have established.

IT'S TOTALLY COPPA AND FERPA COMPLIANT

It's Safe!: Canva is both COPPA and FERPA compliant, so you don't have to worry about the safety of your students. You will need to acquire parental permission for students under 13, but I haven't had issues with this in the past. Just draft a letter explaining its power and how you intend to use it! If your district adopts this platform then you won't have to worry about seeking parent permission. I have started a Facebook group called The Canva Classroom where you can find a letter, documents and other templates to download for use.

CANVA FOR EDUCATION
FEATURES AND FUNCTIONS

SWITCH TEAM	When you create your Canva account, you can create multiple classes. The switch teams button allows you to view each class you have created, and also your personal Canva account or any Canva teams or classes you have joined.
CLASS	When you join Canva for Education, a class will be created and ready for you to invite students and other co-teachers. You can create a class for each subject, period, block, or grade that you teach. You can even just have one if you want. It is up to you!
CLASSWORK	The classwork tab is where all student work that is ready to be reviewed or graded will show up. Classwork can be filtered by work that needs approval, approved, or needs changes.
SHARE WITH TEACHER	This is a student feature that allows students to send work to the teacher when it needs to be reviewed.
NOTIFICATIONS	Notifications are where you will be notified of any activity; comments, work sent to teacher, designs shared directly with you and more.
PEOPLE	People is where you can view all the members that are a part of each team or class. You can change their role from student to co-teacher.
GROUPS	Groups lets you share designs and folders to multiple people at once. This can be students, faculty members or whoever. This is great way to differentiate!
FOLDERS	Folders allow you and students to organize your work by topic, class, or whatever tag you want to give them. This is a good way for students to create portfolios and for the teacher to share multiple documents at once.
NEW ACTIVITY	When in the classwork tab, you can add new activities for students, create from blank, or use the templates provided.
TEMPLATES	Canva has thousands of customizable educational templates to choose from
LMS INTEGRATIONS	On the Billings and Team page, you can enable LMS integrations so you can import students and share assignments directly to your LMS.

INVITING STUDENTS COULDN'T BE EASIER!

Inviting students to your Canva Classroom is easy. You can either post a link for students to join directly in your LMS, or you can go to the people section of your account and invite them by their email address. They recently added a code invite option as well. If you have multiple classes ,you will need to create each team or group and find the invite link for each class. You can also put them all in one team/class, but for organizational purposes I recommend separating them by class, subject, or grade as it makes it easier to filter, review, and collect student work.

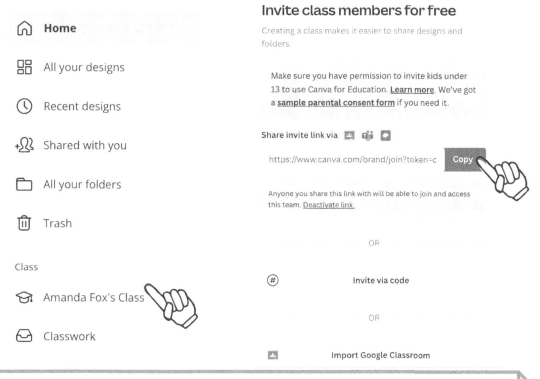

PRO TIP: IF A STUDENT ALREADY HAS AN ACCOUNT, THEY WILL BE ABLE TO NAVIGATE BETWEEN THEIR PERSONAL AND CLASS ACCOUNT IN THE CLASS SETTINGS. MAKE SURE THEY ARE IN YOUR CLASS BEFORE THEY START CREATING TO MANAGE SHARING AND WORKFLOW.

CREATING MULTIPLE CLASSES

When you initially sign up for Canva for Education, one class is created in your teacher dashboard. If you share the join link with all your students they will all be lumped into this one class. This can become cumbersome if you have 100+ students and it can be difficult to search through multiple assignments from multiple classes. In order to manage student work, feedback, and to easily share specific assignments directly with individual classes, I set up and name my classes by periods. You can accomplish this in four easy steps!

1 Step One: To start go click on the gear icon to access account settings.

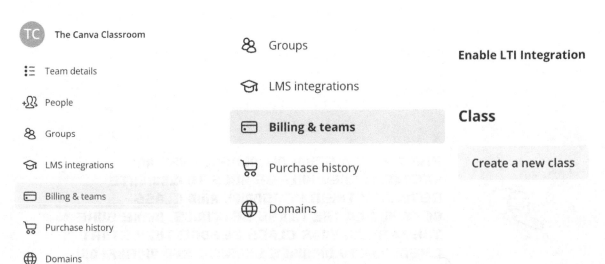

2 Step Two: Click on the billings and team tab.

3 Step Three Click on the 'Create a new class'

TC **The Canva Classroom**

- Team details
- People
- Groups
- LMS integrations
- Billing & teams
- Purchase history
- Domains

- Groups
- LMS integrations
- **Billing & teams**
- Purchase history
- Domains

Enable LTI Integration

Class

Create a new class

Step Four: After clicking 'create a new class' a screen will pop up asking you to give more information about that class. You will name the class and then decide whether or not you want to moderate those that join. I choose not to, so I don't get a thousand notifications. If they have the link and are a member of my domain, it will automatically approve them. After you hit 'create new class' your account will take you back to the main dashboard with suggestions of how you can use Canva with your students.

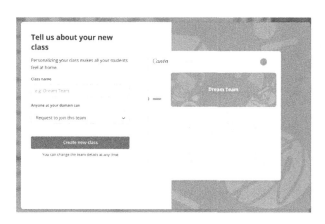

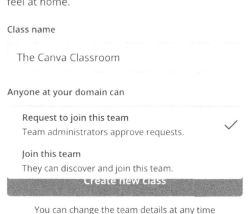

Tell us about your new class

Personalizing your class makes all your students feel at home.

Class name

The Canva Classroom

Anyone at your domain can

Request to join this team ✓
Team administrators approve requests.

Join this team
They can discover and join this team.

Create new class

You can change the team details at any time

Create and learn with your studen ✕

Create and learn with your students on Canva!

It's free to get your students creating on Canva. Invite your students to your class so you can:

- Keep all your students' work in one location

- Easily share learning materials and create assignments

- Let students work together on projects in Canva

- Easily connect work back to your LMS

- Give fun, interactive feedback right in Canva

- Encourage them to develop skills in a safe space

CANVA PLATFORM

FEATURES

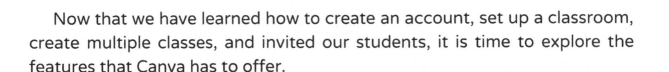

Now that we have learned how to create an account, set up a classroom, create multiple classes, and invited our students, it is time to explore the features that Canva has to offer.

To learn how to navigate the platform, let's start by looking around the 'home' dashboard. There are various clickable options available in the menu bar at the top of the page. There is a square search box that asks what type of product you will design with suggestions below it, and then there is an option menu along the left hand side of the page that gives you access to all of the designs you have created and all of the designs that have been shared with you. Rule of thumb is if you are going to create or seek tutorial videos use the top menu and square in the middle. If you are looking for your designs or designs that your students have created or shared with you, you will look at the menu on the left. If you scroll down, you will also find all of your recent designs. Refer to the image on the next page for a visual.

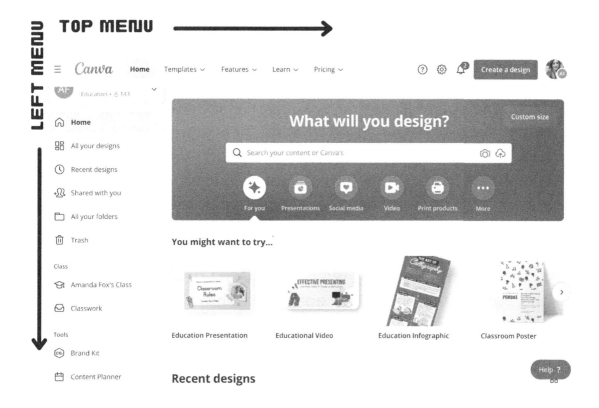

The first thing I want to highlight is the 'Learn' tab. This tab has been a wonderful resource for courses, tutorials, and blogs. Everything you need will teach you how to use each of the features inside!

The courses are also great for introducing students to design basics and they are broken into 1-2 minute easy digestible chunks! And again! They are completely free. I highly recommend the "Design Basics" course for you and your students prior to venturing into creating your first blank canvas. There are also some great educational blogs that highlight Canva use specifically for the classroom. The 'Learn' tab combined with this book and The Canva Classroom facebook page is a sure way to successfully launch your Canva Classroom.

The next option is the feature tab, which essentially gives you the types of designs you can create; a poster, mug, t-shirt, icons, etc. I don't use this search option often. I find the template tab to be my go to. When you click on the template, the option to search by subject, classroom decor, or things you may like pops up. I have used the subject search to browse the templates that relate to my content area. Sometimes I find a template that will act as a launch pad for something I want to design, and other times I just type a keyword into the search bar. For example, I typed in 'Black History Month' and a bunch of templates came back in multiple formats; videos, images, poster, social media posts. There is really a lot of content to search from. Literally, thousands of templates! Don't get too bogged down in finding the perfect template. The goal is to find a starting point and remix.

Social Media	Personal	Business	Marketing	Education
Instagram Stories	Invitations	Presentations	Posters	Classroom Kits
Instagram Posts	Cards	Websites	Flyers	Lesson Plans
Facebook Posts	Resumes	Logos	Infographics	Worksheets
Facebook Covers	Postcards	Business Cards	Brochures	Certificates
YouTube Channel Art	Weekly Schedule Pla...	Invoice	Newsletters	Bookmarks
LinkedIn Banners	T-Shirts	Business Letterheads	Proposals	Class Schedules

Education Presentations   Educational Videos   Education Infographics   Classroom Posters   Google Classroom Headers

Browse by Subject

Marketing   Business   Math   Design   Science

CANVA FOR EDUCATION FEATURES AND FUNCTIONS

Once you decide on a template, whether it's a video, social post, infographic or whatever else you choose, it's time to customize it! Instead of writing a paragraph on each dashboard feature, I am going to provide a quick reference guide of customization options. The best way to learn is through play! Let's start creating!

ELEMENTS	This is where you will find a reservoir of stock photos, graphics, animations, videos, and audio to add to your design.
UPLOADS	You can upload videos, audio, or images from your computer, Facebook, Google Drive, Google Photos, Instagram, or Dropbox. More options are being added all the time. You can also find anything you previously uploaded here.
PHOTOS	Photos brings up images you recently used, magic recommendations based on something you have selected that you like, and also shows trending photos in the platform. You can search by textures, gradients, borders, backgrounds, and more.
TEXT	Text allows you to add headings, subheadings and body text styles to your document, and it also brings up a font filter and size. You can also go to effects and curve your text and add highlights. There are a bunch of font combinations for typography noobs.
VIDEOS	While you can search for videos in the elements section, this filter lets you choose by aerial shots, nature, potential backgrounds. and many other topics.
ALL DESIGNS	You can find everything you have created in Canva here. If you want to combine designs you can open up a previous design and click here to add a former design to the page.

VIDEO AND PHOTO EDITING FEATURES AND FUNCTIONS

ONLINE VIDEO RECORDER	Record yourself while presenting. There are two ways: through uploads and 'record myself,' or 'present and record.' Share it via a video link with students, friends, or colleagues, or even PDs for easy watching. You can even check out the stats on views!
VIDEO TRIMMER	To change the length of your video click on the video you want to edit then select 'trim' in the editor tool bar. Drag the blue sliders to select the new length of the video. You're done!
RESIZE AND CROP VIDEO	After you select the video you want to resize or crop, click on the white dots in the corner of the video to resize it. You can also crop the video by selecting 'crop' in the toolbar above the editor, or by double clicking.
ANIMATION	You can add animations to your designs by clicking the animation button. You can animate the whole page with page animations, or each item or text individually.
EDIT IMAGE FILTERS	With edit image, you can auto focus, auto enhance, adjust the brightness, contract and add filter effects all within the platform.
FRAMES	With frames you can reshape or crop an image by adding a frame to a design and then dragging the image inside of it.
ADD TEXT	You can add your own text to images and designs in Canva by selecting the text element. Then customize the text to what you want.
EDIT TEXT	You can change the color, size, and also add text effects such as curved text, glow, shadows, and more.
BACKGROUND REMOVER	Remove the background from images with one click. Wait for the background to be processed and then fine tune your editing with the erase and restore brush.
FLIP	Use the Flip feature on the toolbar to flip images horizontally or vertically.
TRANSPARENCY	Adjust the transparency of items in your design by clicking on the item and then selecting the transparency checkerboard icon. Click and slide the dot until you are happy with your design.

SHORT CUTS AND CREATE OPTIONS

The awesome slides below were created by @Colb_hawk.

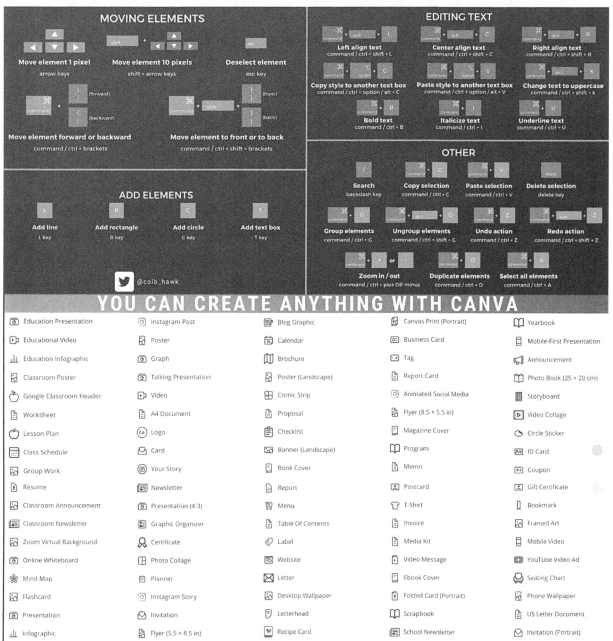

CANVA AND VIDEO

Canva has a ton of video templates and stock videos available to enhance presentations and designs. One of my favorite Canva features is the Canva Video Recording tool (and the Canva video templates). Prior to Canva I used Google slides to create presentations and then either import them to another platform or use another tool to add video to them; Swivl, Screencastify, iMovie, and Camtasia being the primary tools of choice. With Canva I am given multiple ways to create video enhanced designs, and I can share the video easily by posting a link in my LMS or sharing directly to a class inside of Canva. You could also choose to download it and then upload it to Youtube or another social media platform. There are two main ways you can record and add video to your templates: 'Present and Record', and 'Record Yourself.' I will cover both ways to use the video feature, including how they differ and when to use each function (there is also the option to upload videos you have directly into a design).

PRESENT AND RECORD

When a design is open, you can click on the three dots in the top right hand corner of the platform and then find the 'present and record' feature. This will bring up an option to go to the recording studio. You will need to make sure you have selected the correct camera and microphone when you enter the studio. You can even filter your videos!

Inside of the studio, you will find slide deck thumbnails in the bottom of the frame, and the current presentation slide is large and in the center. There is a section for notes on the right hand side. As you record you are also given the option to pause your video. I don't know about you, but I struggle to talk through an entire presentation flawlessly. This allows me to pause between slides and recollect my thoughts. A truly helpful feature is the timer in the upper left corner. I try to keep my flipped lectures to a certain length and this helps me monitor my time and be more concise. To go to the next slide you simply click on the one you want to talk about next. When you are finished presenting, you simply hit 'end recording' and it will upload your video to the presentation and combine them. Your video will manifest as a small circle in the left hand corner of the presentation. When you create designs made for videos be mindful to leave space on the design for your small circle.

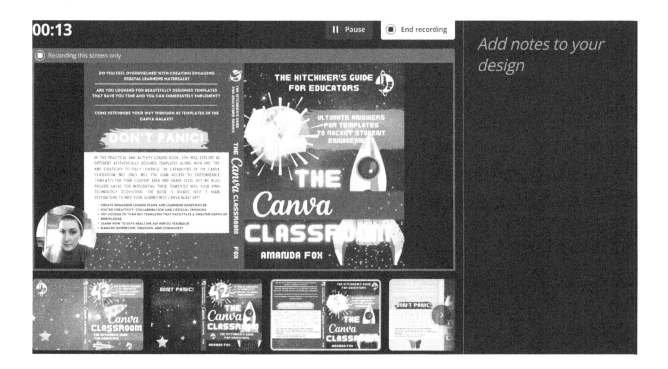

PROTIP: THE FIRST TIME I CREATED A PRESENT AND RECORD VIDEO THE VIDEO CIRCLE COVERED UP PARTS OF MY PRESENTATION, SO BE MINDFUL OF THIS WHEN DESIGNING AND BE SURE NOT TO ADD ANY CRUCIAL TEXT OR INFORMATION IN THIS SPOT.

You can generate a link to share the presentation with peers, or students, but again you can also download the video to post elsewhere. The video will continue to be a part of the file unless you decide to delete it or record over it. The 'present and record' feature can be used with all Canva designs! It doesn't have to be a video template to work.

I can create a presentation and add video via the Canva Recording Studio by hitting 'Present and Record'. With remote learning being the norm the past few years I used this method a lot to record instructions on top of templates and assignments that I created for students, and also for flipped lectures. I then share, and it doesn't matter who did or didn't show up to the zoom call, or was in-class that day. There have even been times that I haven't had time to pre-record instructions, so I have hit record while going over the activity live.This is a great way to disseminate the same information to all students, and it solves the question "what are we supposed to do again?" or "what did you do when I was out?"

RECORD MYSELF

The second way to add video to a design is by hitting the 'upload tab' in the left hand corner of the platform. From here there are two ways to use this option: you can upload a preexisting video that you have on your computer, or you can hit 'record yourself'. Since this section is all about the Canva video tool, I'm only going to discuss the latter.

Once you enter the recording studio it offers an additional option that 'present and record' does not. You have the option to record video and a screen share of either a website, or other window you have open on your computer. For explainer videos and tutorials the screen share option is fantastic.

Another way this differs from 'Present and Record' is that the video is not in a small circle on your screen. It loads as a regular square video that is resizable and can be moved to different parts of the presentation. Instead of having one continuous talking presentation with the same video you have the option to add multiple videos to each slide. To make it more aesthetic there are different frames you can add to the video depending on the tone, nature, and objective to the design. If you search 'video frame' in the elements or photo section you will find a ton of ways to anchor the video aesthetically.

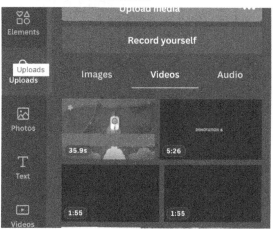

BUILD A WEBSITE

Websites can be of value in the educational context, whether we are designing a classroom website, a school website, or students are creating digital resumes or portfolios. Creating a website in Canva is as easy as clicking the 'Share tab' and then selecting 'Website'. Once you hit 'Publish' your designs will instantly turn into a functional website. You can select classic website functionality like navigation, scrolling, presentation and standard designs.

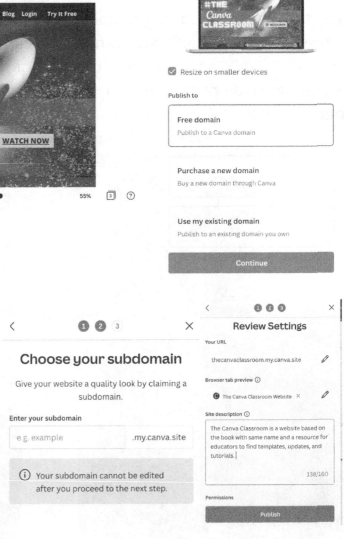

When it comes to domain hosting, you can use a free domain provided by Canva, purchase one through Canva, or connect an existing domain you already own. If you go the free route, which I did, you do get to pick a subdomain. You hit continue, then write a short description of the website. You can password protect it, which is great for classroom privacy! For more ideas on how to use the Website feature, check out th template section!

DESTINATION THREE: OUT OF THIS WORLD TEACHING, ASSESSMENT AND FEEDBACK

"OH MY GOODNESS, WATCHING THE CHILDREN COLLABORATE AND DEVELOP THOSE 21ST CENTURY SKILLS ON CANVA HAS BEEN EXTRAORDINARY! I HAVE THOROUGHLY ENJOYED WATCHING THE UNIQUE IDEAS THAT THE CHILDREN COME UP WITH. WATCHING THEIR MINDS WORK AS THEY CREATE SOMETHING TOTALLY NEW! NOT SOMETHING THEY HAVE BEEN ASKED TO ADD TO OR TWEAK. I NOW USE CANVA ON MY CLASS NOTEBOOK, ON MY DISPLAYS, AS A WAY FOR CHILDREN TO CREATE A RESPONSE TO QUESTIONS, A COLLABORATION TOOL THAT CAN THEN BE PRESENTED! THE OPTIONS ARE LIMITLESS. ALONG WITH THE INTEGRATION OF FLIPGRID! I LOVE EVERY MINUTE WITH CANVA AND SO DO THE CHILDREN IN MY CLASS."

-CATHERINE COLEMAN, 5TH GRADE TEACHER, RICHMOND ACADEMY FOR THE STOUR ACADEMY TRUST

BUILDING A BRAND FOR YOUR CLASSROOM, SCHOOL, OR DISTRICT

By this point you should have a pretty good feel for the Canva platform, how to create classes, invite students, and all of the features and apps that are at your fingertips. In this chapter I am going to cover how to create a classroom brand. If you are using Canva for building a classroom brand, creating social media posts, newsletters, decor, and student assignments this chapter will help you take advantage of the brand feature. As an elementary classroom teacher this will allow you to preset fonts for handwriting, and as a district technologist, or admin, it will ensure that your school colors and logos are always just a click away.

BUILDING A CLASSROOM BRAND WITH CANVA

Creating a classroom theme or brand is a huge market. If you go to TeachersPayTeachers you can purchase pre-made posters, banners, worksheets, and pretty much any classroom decor by searching for a theme or topic you are interested in. I want to start by saying not branding or theming your classroom is also ok. Having a perfect Pinterest classroom doesn't determine if you are a good teacher. It is the experiences that you facilitate in your classroom that lead to learning and student success that truly matter. However, themes can be fun for units, and activities, and they don't necessarily have to extend to everything you do. They also build a sense of community in your classroom and share your interests with your students. I have personally found it easier when creating designs to have a brand kit set up with my preferred fonts, and hex colors preloaded, so I don't have to recreate the wheel. You can use the 'brand kit' feature to populate this. One of my favorite themes to use in my classroom is a 'Stranger Things' theme. I teach middle school and high school, and by decorating and designing lessons in theme it allows me to immediately begin relationship building.

If you are a district or admin, then the brand feature is almost a necessity for professional development, school newsletters, and communications. Check out my 'Stranger Things' classroom decor, and lessons around themed vocabulary activity!

STRANGER THINGS VOCABULARY DECK

CHOOSING COLORS

If you are a minimalist teacher, you may opt out of doing a classroom theme and choose to stick to colors and fonts that work for you and your students. It may be based on school colors or just preference. When writing and designing the layout for this book, having these predetermined was a huge time saver! Let's start by selecting colors. First you will select 'brand kit.' Next, you simply pick colors that you like. If you have a mascot, or graphic with the colors you want to use, you can cheat by using the color picker tool to find out what the HEX code is for each color. Hex color is short for hexadecimal and is a type of HTML color code that starts with a # and is followed by a six digit number value. It is valuable when creating continuity between designs and brand materials. After you have your codes, write them down, and go into 'brand kit' and add them to your color palette. I usually have multiple brand kits saved. I have one for this book, another for a video game unit I create, and then another with school colors and fonts for designing newsletters.

CHOOSING FONTS

When it comes to fonts, your choices may be guided by the age group that you teach. For example, if creating worksheets or posters for primary and elementary students you will want to choose a font that is easy for them to learn letters and begin to read. You may want to create a second brand kit for designing handwriting worksheets that includes traceable fonts. Regardless of your age group, the rule of thumb is you shouldn't have more than three types of fonts in a document or design. The brand kit feature actually limits you to three fonts; a heading, subheading, and body. You can even upload fonts that you find on the internet. You will just need to check the copyright and make sure your usage falls within the perimeters of permissions. I uploaded "Beauty School DropOut" as the main heading font for chapters. Now that you have your brand kit set up let's get into the best strategies for teaching using Canva Designs.

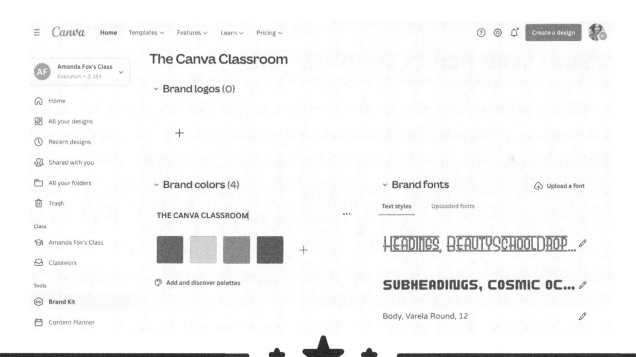

"USING THE BRAND KIT TO CREATE A GROUP OF FONTS THAT ARE PERFECT FOR HANDWRITING WORKSHEETS AND SAVES TIME!"

CANVA LOGOS FOR CLASSROOM USE

Now that you have your colors and fonts, you can use the logo feature to create a classroom logo. Logos are great to add to your Google Classroom headers, posters, newsletters, and welcome signs. If you sponsor a club or a sport, you can also create logos for these as well. When I taught film, I would have loved to have this feature for students to create their own production studio logos! Last year, I taught a marketing unit and students had to create logos for their marketing firms. Getting students involved in logo creation is a great design exercise that is quick, and also a great project to teach design principles.

When creating a logo, you can work from an educational template, or create a logo from scratch. With Bitmoji integration right into the Canva platform, it allows teachers to use their avatars in their logo designs. You select Bitmoji from the available apps, connect your account, and then add your avatar to the design! Another way I have seen educators use the logo feature is to create classroom achievement badges. Badges are a fantastic way to award student success and progress. Here are a few examples below.

Classroom Logo   Student Created Designs   Pathway Badges

TEACHING WITH CANVA

10

Chapters three through five covered how to design a good lesson starting with DOK and asking good questions to design tasks, using the Understanding by Design framework, paying attention to design principles and aesthetics, and ensuring designs are inclusive of students using the Universal Design Framework. In this section I am going to go more in depth on the types of instructional strategies you can facilitate using Canva apps, integrations, and tools. Our instructional strategies should be diverse and reflect the students that are in our classroom. Canva enables teachers to create multimodal content to reach every student where they are via video presentations, slide decks, infographics, and flipped videos to name a few. It also makes sharing designs with our classroom easy and streamlined depending on our strategy and environment. Teachers have the option for traditional in person instruction using the present feature, or using Canva.Live for interactive back channels. Designs can also be shared virtually by posting them to Google Classroom, or assigning them to your students within the Canva educator dashboard.

On the next few pages, we will explore tools and designs we can create for our classroom environments and also teacher-centered instructional materials to aid in instruction and hopefully spark innovative ideas! I know each time I search the Canva database for educator designed templates I either find something I can remix or come up with something novel to create. You can filter templates based on what type of assignment you are creating, by subject, theme, and grade level. Let's explore!

DESIGNS FOR YOUR CLASSROOM

The following chart shares examples of teacher created designs you can use in your classroom. Scan the QR Codes to get access to the templates and customize them for your personal use.

GOOGLE HEADER	Google headers are a great way to customize your Google Classroom and Google Forms. Create a new design for each class to visually differentiate between them. You can even make animated headers by adding text and graphic animations and then downloading the header as a gif. You can create headers for your personal and classroom Twitter accounts as well.
CLASS SCHEDULE	Class schedules are awesome for sharing the structure of the day. You can make these as detailed or as simple as you like. When my students were remote learning, I created a schedule for the month which included links to Nearpod lessons, Canva templates, and Edpuzzle videos. This gave them one document to refer to and communicated daily expectations, due dates, and which assignments were graded.
CLUB FLYERS	With Canva you can create flyers to send home or post around the school to keep everyone informed on things that are going on. My students created a flyer with a QR code to a survey. The template here is for an Esports club with information on how to sign up!
QR CODE BATHROOM SIGN OUT	Make your classroom sign out sheets digital by adding a QR code to a Google Form, adding to your design, printing it, and posting them by your door! Simply make a class drop down roster for all of your classes, and have them scan it when leaving and returning to the room. You have a timestamp of each student's activity in and out of the classroom.
NEWSLETTER TO PARENTS	You can generate letters home quickly with the variety of newsletters Canva has to offer. This template is for a supply list for design challenges, and asks parents to volunteer to donate materials to classroom. You can also create weekly newsletters or classroom announcements.

INSTRUCTIONAL STRATEGIES USING CANVA TEMPLATES

HYPERDOCS

Hyperdocs are essentially digital lesson plans designed by teachers that organize content and learning into one template. You can add hyperlinks, videos, and embed content into the template for students to learn about a topic. You can even have them apply this information inside the template itself! Check out this hyperdoc on Parts of Speech!

PARTS OF SPEECH

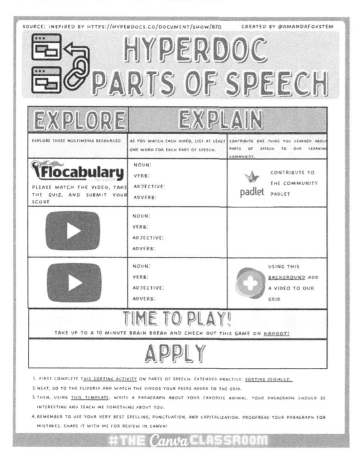

SCAN FOR HYPERDOC

The hyperdoc to the left is broken down into explore, explain, practice/play, and apply.

It leverages Kahoot, Flipgrid, Flocabulary, Padlet, Canva templates, Genially, and Youtube videos.

FLIPPING YOUR CLASSROOM

Flipped lessons supply students with information to review prior to class time, so class time can be spent applying the content. You can share a video presentation, slide deck, or other informational content to students to review on their own. If you aren't ready to flip your classroom, you can always do an in-flip. An in-flip is when you show the video in class. The benefit is that you ensure every class receives the same content and are free to float and help those that need it. Below is a flipped video on presidential vs parliamentary democracy.

SCAN FOR FLIPPED TEMPLATE

AUDIO/VIDEO INSTRUCTIONS

What are we doing again? You can add audio and video instructions to any lesson or activity by going to 'upload' and record myself. This is a fantastic way to leverage the UDL framework to ensure you are representing information in multiple modes, and it helps communicate student expectations.

SCAN FOR EXAMPLE

PEAR DECK + CANVA INTERACTIVE LESSONS

Pear Deck lessons created with Canva are a great way to actively engage students while you are delivering instructional content. This allows for real time formative feedback with multiple options to add interactivity to your lessons! In the next chapter, App Integrations, I will go in more detail on how you can app smash using Canva and Pear Deck.

SCAVENGER HUNTS

Scavenger hunts can be a great way to engage your students and promote collaboration while combining the digital and physical worlds. They are great for physical classrooms or remote learning, and synchronous or asynchronous instruction. 'About Me' scavenger hunts can facilitate building relationships and community in your classroom by asking students to add images to a pre-made template. You can also create digital scavenger hunts by adding hyperlinks to websites and asking them a question about that site. They can share answers in the form of screenshots, videos, images, or text. Check out the examples below.

IDEAS FOR SCAVENGER HUNTS

- About Me
- Math in Real Life
- History Scavenger Hunt
- Simple Machines Scavenger Hunt
- SEL Scavenger Hunt
- Sight Word Scavenger Hunt

SIMPLE MACHINES SCAVENGER HUNT

In this scavenger hunt, students label the simple machines, and then they have to go find them in real life!! Check out the augmented reality coloring page of the ferris wheel from Quiver Vision, a wheel and axel machine, from the kid's book, Markertown. This template can also be modified to find geometric shapes, sight words, colors, etc.

SCAN THE QR CODE FOR THE TEMPLATE

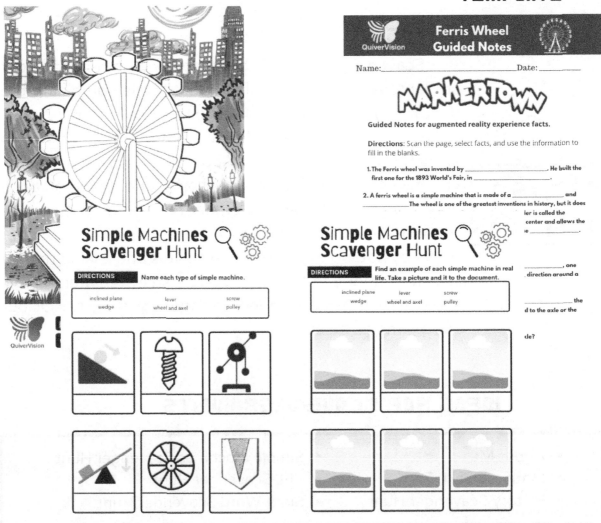

BITMOJI CLASSROOMS

Bitmoji classrooms have been all the rage, and in Canva you can easily make them! If you search 'virtual classroom' there are over 30 templates to choose from. If you don't find exactly what you are looking for, you can also import any images you want to use. With the Bitmoji app integrated with Canva, it makes it super easy to import your avatars into a template. You can use this to introduce yourself to students, create daily agendas, and even deliver content. You can add hyperlinks to text, images, and even videos. Check out the examples below!

THE SOCRATIC RAVEN

SCAN FOR ACCESS TO A MEET THE TEACHER BITMOJI CLASSROOM

MEET THE TEACHER

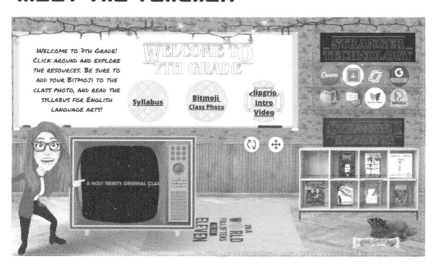

CHECK OUT ESCAPE ED
BY BRIAN COSTELLO

DIGITAL BREAKOUTS & CANVA ESCAPE ROOMS

Breakouts are a way to gamify content in your classroom and make learning more fun. Breakouts have students practice critical thinking and deductive reasoning. Skills that are important for the workforce!

Breakouts involve riddles or clues that students are prompted to solve. They put learning back into the hands of the students, while the teacher, or game maker, facilitates on the side providing hints when necessary.

Digital breakouts are a great way to leverage critical thinking and problem solving in the classroom. Students can work individually or collaboratively to solve puzzles and unlock locks to solve or escape the room. You can use the Canva website builder feature, or a virtual or Bitmoji classroom filled with clues that students have to figure out.

You can create one for any content area and use any theme that will engage your students. You may want to include other websites and resources in your breakout. You can create locks using google forms and add them to your Canva website or template as well. Anything that can be linked can be added, so it is really up to your imagination! Check out the next page for 24 different tools you can link or embed in your Canva breakout!

24 DIGITAL BREAKOUT TOOLS

CREATED BY @AMANDAFOXSTEM

LINK TO CANVA DIGITAL BREAKOUT TEMPLATE

LINK TO CANVA ESCAPE ROOM EXPERIENCE

GENIALLY INTERACTIVE IMAGE

FAKE RECEIPT

FAKE SOCIAL MEDIA ACCOUNT

SECRET MESSAGE SNOTE

THINGLINK 360 IMAGE

GOOGLE FORMS

JIGSAW PLANET

CANVA WEBSITE

FAKE CONCERT TICKETS

FAKE TEXT MESSAGES

FAKE AIRPLANE TICKETS

FAKE PASSPORT

FAKE NEWSPAPER ARTICLE

FAKE WHATSAPP MESSAGE

REBUS PUZZLE

HIDE WORDS IN A MANDALA

HIDESEE.COM RED LENS VIEWER

EYE CHART MAKER

MORSE CODE GENERATOR

BINARY CODE CONVERTER

FAKE CHECK GENERATOR

STREET SIGN GENERATOR

GEO GREETING

HIEROGLYPIC TRANSLATOR

#THE Canva CLASSROOM

CANVA VIRTUAL ESCAPE ROOM

SCAN ME

CANVA DIGITAL BREAKOUT
WEBSITE TEMPLATE

The templates provided on this page will help you jump start breakouts with Canva in your classroom. Scan the QR codes to start making one now!

SCAN ME

EDGAR ALLAN POE DIGITAL BREAKOUT FROM BREAKOUTEDU--USES CANVA

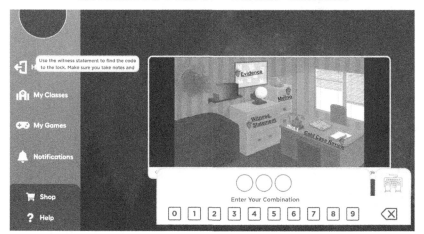

DIGITAL BREAK OUT ON DIGITAL CITIZENSHIP CREATED BY MELISSA SULLIVAN!

Melissa Sullivan is an educator that connected with me on Twitter. Here is an example of an awesome breakout she made on digital citizenship.

MADE IN *Canva*

MYSTERY CARDS FOR BREAKOUT ROOMS

BY RYAN READ

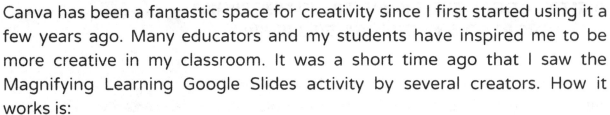

Canva has been a fantastic space for creativity since I first started using it a few years ago. Many educators and my students have inspired me to be more creative in my classroom. It was a short time ago that I saw the Magnifying Learning Google Slides activity by several creators. How it works is:

Open Canva and Choose your Template such as a card or flier. Then it is about creating a template that comes in the layers and the colors used. The answer on each slide is typed in the same exact color as the background so that it looks invisible.

So the layers are really:

Choose your background (in the very back)
Create or Import a magnifying glass clipart piece (in the middle)
Select the text and put in the mystery answer (on the top-most layer)
This is how you are suddenly able to see the answer – because the words are actually appearing on top of the light-colored magnifying glass and are no longer camouflaged by the same-color background.

There are many ways you might utilize this template in Canva for your classroom

A mystery card can be used to:

- Reveal answers from math problems solved with partners
- Uncover answers after completing a reading comprehension with a small group
- Learn new vocabulary through repetitive practice
- Have hidden clues for Breakout EDU Games
- Review important facts
- Complete math fact practice
- Create Site Word Challenges
- Create Wordle Games such as how many words can you spell with the hidden letters

SCAN TO GET
MYSTERY CARDS
TEMPLATE

SCAN TO WATCH
VIDEO ON MYSTERY
CARDS

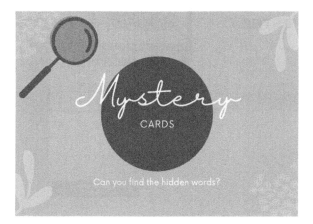

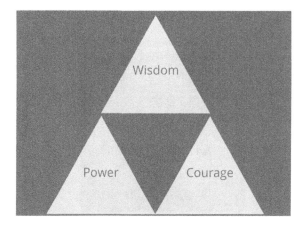

CANVA.LIVE PRESENTATION

The Canva.Live feature is a hidden gem in Canva! You can launch a Canva.Live presentation while presenting to an audience and it allows you to interact with your audience via a backchannel and hot keys. You simply open a design or presentation and select 'present.' At the bottom of the presentation view you will be given the option to start a new Canva Live session and a 6-digit code will be generated. Students will visit Canva.live in their browser and enter the code to ask questions while you present. You can visit other tabs and browsers outside of the presentation and the live session will continue until you click 'end,' while in presentation mode. This is a great option for students to ask questions, make comments, and provide feedback to you while you present. I have found students that don't usually raise their hand in class use more readily engage in the classroom. There are also hot keys that you can use while you are presenting! This is also a great option for professional development sessions. Remember back channel? Maybe not, but it had the same premise, except it's embedded directly into Canva!

Check out the awesome graphic on the next page contributed by Colby Hawkins, @Colb_hawk, digital learning specialist in JSD, Utah.

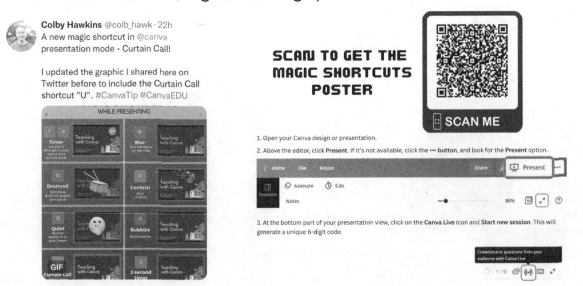

Canva
MAGIC SHORTCUTS
WHILE PRESENTING

 1 through **9**

Timer
use keys 1 through 9 insert one to nine minute timer

 B

Blur
Blur the focus on the slide

 D

Drumroll
Start/Stop drumroll graphic and sound

C

Confetti
Start confetti

 Q

Quiet
Prompt audience to quiet down

 O

Bubbles
Start bubbles

 U

Curtain Call
Open / close curtain on the slide

 **M**

Mic Drop
Start/Stop mic drop

 0

3 second timer
zero key for 3 second timer

HAPPY PRESENTING! 🐦 @colb_hawk
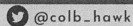

CREATING LEARNING STATIONS WITH CANVA

Learning stations in the classroom are physical spaces where students are asked to work individually or in a group to work on learning objectives. They are a great way to differentiate by student voice, choice, path, and pace. For example, regarding student choice, you could create stations that address the same standard but have students communicate their knowledge in a different way. In a physical setting, activity cards, or task cards are set up in each station and students work through the activities, then rotate.

The example I am providing is a STEM Literacy station around the book Markertown. After students read the book, they rotate through the various stations and complete the activity on the station cards. The cards were created in Canva, but aren't centered around collecting student work in Canva (though you could have Canva specific stations if desired). There is a 'build a playground station,' 'design a scribble bot,' 'spray art,' and 'design a finger puppet' station. At the end of the rotations, students are prompted to fill out a reflection card of the stations they participated in as a self-assessment activity. The template for these cards is available for remixing on the next page.

TEMPLATE TO STATION CARDS

Stations can also be facilitated virtually through Zoom or Google Meet breakouts. You can create questions in a Canva Hyperdoc or choice board and have students break into small groups to address a different question. Simply share the template link or an edit link if they are collaborating together, and assign them to a breakout room. You can monitor student progress of all groups by opening each design in Canva.

Now that you have some ideas of how to integrate Canva into your daily teaching, let's move on learn how to assign designs to students!

JOIN MY FACEBOOK GROUP!

Have you you joined my group on Facebook yet? Pop in and tell me what you think of the book so far, and share any ideas you have for using Canva!!

SCAN ME

CREATING AND ASSIGNING A DESIGN TO STUDENTS

We set up our Canva for Education classes in chapter seven. If you haven't created your classes yet, you will need to revisit that section and be sure to follow the instructions prior to creating an assignment. It is recommended to create multiple classes if you teach different grade levels or content areas. This keeps everything organized and easy to find when you have a lot of students. If you teach elementary and have only one class of the same students this is an unnecessary step.

To quickly recap how to create another class, you will go up to the settings tab and click on it, find 'billings and teams' on the left side dashboard, and select 'create a new class.' To toggle back and forth between your various classes you will simply click on your icon in the top right corner and select the class you want to assign a template to.

An easy way to visually differentiate between classes is to create a unique banner for each one. You can do this by clicking on the three dots on your classroom graphic and selecting 'create banner' and then customize it for each class. When you are finished creating a custom banner, click 'update teams banner' and the new banner will populate. Keep in mind your classroom name will remain on the interior of the banner, so when you create your design plan for a space in the middle of the design.

GENERIC BANNER

CUSTOM BANNER

ASSIGNING TEMPLATES TO STUDENTS

Once you have your classes set up and are ready to create your first assignment, you will need to pick a template that you want to push to students. You can lock any of the elements you do not want students to have the ability to change, allowing them only to edit text input or elements they will need to manipulate through drag and drop. There are multiple ways to assign templates and activities depending on if it is an individual assignment, group work, or a collaborative assignment the whole class will work on. Next, let's look at each type of assignment and the best way to assign it based on the assignment type.

INDIVIDUAL ASSIGNMENT

To assign a template to students will start by clicking on the three dots in the top right hand corner of your screen. You will be given recommended options of how to share the assignment. The easiest way to assign an individual template to students is to click on the assignment tab. You can add instructions prior to assigning the template, and then choose the correct class to assign it to. Next, click 'publish.' This will share the assignment directly in Canva with each student in that class. Students will be notified of a new assignment.

1.CLICK ON THE THREE DOTS

2.SELECT 'ASSIGNMENT'

4. WRITE INSTRUCTIONS

3.SHARE TO CANVA

5. SHARE TO CLASS + PUBLISH

If you have an LMS like Google Classroom or Microsoft Teams, it may be easier for students to manage due dates and activities by assigning it through your LMS. If you choose Google Classroom it will open up 'create an assignment' portal within Google Classroom, and you will choose the classroom you want to assign it to as well as instructions, a due date, points, and the option to also tag it with a topic. If you have not synced your LMS with Canva, you can also click on the 'share' button at the top of your dashboard, and change the type of sharing to 'template.' You then copy the link and post it in your LMS, and it will create a copy for each individual student. You can also follow the steps above and instead of selecting 'Canva' you will select your LMS and hit publish. Examples of individual assignments are vocabulary practice, worksheets, or graphic organizers.

GROUP WORK

There are also multiple ways to assign a template to predetermined groups or teams. The first way is assigning the groups within Canva. You will need to make multiple copies of the template and name them "Group1-Assignment Title', and so on. You will go into each template and go to the 'share' button and type in the students names that are members of that class you wish to share the template with. You will do this for each template. Each group will only have access to the template you shared with them. You will still be the owner of the document and will be able to monitor their progress by visiting each group's template. This is great for offering feedback during the process.

A second way to push out a group assignment is to share an editable link in your LMS as an assignment. When you create the assignment in Google Classroom or your LMS, you will select the students you wish to share the template with. This will give them access to the document, and you will retain the ability to view the template and their progress as they complete the activity.

Examples of group templates could be presentations, literature circles, and breakout sessions.

1. CLICK ON THE SHARE BUTTON

2. TYPE IN STUDENTS NAMES IN THE GROUP

OR

1. CLICK ON SHARE

2. SHARE A LINK TO EDIT AND COPY

3. POST THE LINK TO GOOGLE CLASSROOM AS AN ASSIGNMENT AND ONLY SHARE TO STUDENTS IN THAT GROUP

WHOLE CLASS COLLABORATIVE ASSIGNMENT

Collaborative assignments for the whole class are great when you are doing a quick formative assessment check, bell ringers, exit tickets, or general concept practice. There are two main ways to give students access to the document. Instead of using Jamboard, I opt to use Canva.

The first way to share is within the Canva platform. All of your designs are private until you make them visible to your class. To share with your class, make sure you are the correct class you wish to share the template with and go to 'share.' This is an alternative option to sharing a design using a link. After you hit share you will click on the eyeball icon to give your class visibility to the template. You will then direct students to go to 'shared designs' in their dashboard to work on the document as a class. The downfall of this option is that it might slip by students if they aren't looking for the assignment. This option is best utilized while you are teaching class in person, and you can direct students where to go. While students should receive a notification that a template has been shared, they aren't always proactively looking for work in the 'shared designs' tab, and it can take a minute to be notified.

The second and preferred option to assign a template for the whole class is to share within your LMS. This is also the best option for online, or hybrid learning, because it is posted to the LMS they have most likely been trained to check for new assignments (however I will be training future classes to check Canva). To provide access for whole class collaborative editing, go to 'share,' change the template setting to 'edit' and copy the link. Post the link to your LMS, and every student will have access to the same document. If you teach multiple classes, you will need to make a copy of the template for each class.

PROTIP: WHEN ASSIGNING WHOLE CLASS COLLABORATIVE TEMPLATES MAKE A SLIDE FOR EACH STUDENT. INCLUDE AN INSTRUCTIONS SLIDE IN THE TEMPLATE THAT EXPLAINS WHAT THE TASK IS.

1.HIT THE SHARE BUTTON

2. HIT THE EYEBALL ICON TO MAKE THE ASSIGNMENT VISIBLE TO THE CLASS

OR

LINK TO COMIC VOCABULARY TEMPLATE

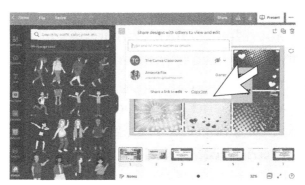

COPY THE LINK AND POST IT IN YOUR LMS AS AN ASSIGNMENT. STUDENTS WILL BE ABLE TO WORK ON THE DESIGN AS A CLASS.

ASSESSMENT AND FEEDBACK IN CANVA

Providing assessment and feedback is an important part of the learning process, but assessment and feedback are not the same thing and should not be used interchangeably. Feedback is information on performance given with the intent to improve that performance. Assessment is a judgment, or deciding the amount, value, quality, or importance of a student's work. The goal of formative assessment is to monitor student learning to provide ongoing feedback that can be used by instructors to improve their teaching and for students to improve their learning. More specifically, formative assessments help students identify their strengths and weaknesses and target areas that need work (Carnegie Mellon University, 2022). When you get down to it, all assessments are formative if you are using the data to target student strengths and needs and using that data to differentiate instruction accordingly. So think of formative, as informative!

Canva can be used for both feedback and assessment. Teacher created graphic organizers, worksheets, bellringers, and exit tickets are all created with the goal of collecting data and analyzing student performance. The platform offers an abundance of opportunities to provide feedback during design creation, and also assess student created work. While this section isn't meant to go in depth on assessing student performance, it IS a guide to the various strategies and tools you can leverage within the Canva platform to help students improve. Let's look at some strategies of how we can use Canva to provide feedback.

PROVIDING FEEDBACK IN CANVA

The first mode of feedback is built right into the Canva platform. You learned how to share assignments with students in the previous section. But how do you get it back to review it and provide feedback? It is pretty simple. After students make edits to the design, or complete the assignment, they then submit it for teacher review by clicking 'Send to teacher'. You'll find all the assignments that students have shared for review under the 'Classwork' tab on the left hand side of your education dashboard. By clicking it you can review the assignments that have been submitted and leave your feedback for the student. One of the nice features is it also shows a timestamp so you can differentiate between assignments that are turned in on time and which ones were late.

My favorite feature in managing feedback and assessment is the 'all approvals' drop down bar at the top of your dashboard that is accessible from the 'classwork' tab. You can sort through work in the 'all approvals' drop down bar to see which students still need to be reviewed, which ones were approved, and which students you sent work back to make adjustments. If you still depend on Google Classroom, Microsoft Teams, or an LMS to distribute assignments and aren't a full blown Canvanaut yet, you can also assign work and grade it through your LMS. Now let's move on to some other creative ways to assess and provide feedback within Canva using other apps and tools!

Class	Classwork		Status	Last update
🎓 Amanda Fox's Class				
✉️ **Classwork**	**All approvals** All classwork	✓	NEEDS REVIEW	10:34 AM, Feb 16
Tools	**Needs review** Classwork which requires approval		NEEDS REVIEW	7:34 PM Feb 9
▦ Discover apps				
🎒 Brand Kit	**Approved** Classwork which has been approved	oy mont	NEEDS REVIEW	1:22 PM Feb 9
📅 Content Planner	**Needs changes** Classwork with changes requested		NEEDS REVIEW	10:52 AM, Feb 9

OTHER CREATIVE WAYS TO PROVIDE FEEDBACK TO STUDENTS IN CANVA

BITMOJI FEEDBACK

The Bitmoji app is conveniently integrated into Canva and there are so many ways to use it. I go over about 10 different ways in the app integrations chapter. One of the ways I love to use it is to drop my Bitmoji into student projects while they are in progress. To do this, I make sure students add my name to all designs as an editor. I schedule check-in days where I drop into their projects and give feedback on where they are. They know I have dropped in when I leave an avatar with a comic call out and feedback. This gives students the opportunity to apply that feedback as they are in the throes of learning and application. It also gives them time prior to the deadline to 'get it right.' Oftentimes, I see teachers who assign projects and then grade them at the very end and that end grade is what students get stuck with due to lack of time to revisit and revise. So give Bitmoji feedback a try! You will be pleasantly surprised at the increase of quality of the final designs and presentations.

OFTENTIMES, I SEE TEACHERS WHO ASSIGN PROJECTS AND THEN GRADE THEM AT THE VERY END AND THAT END GRADE IS WHAT STUDENTS GET STUCK WITH DUE TO LACK OF TIME TO REVISIT AND REVISE. SO GIVE BITMOJI FEEDBACK A TRY! YOU WILL BE PLEASANTLY SURPRISED AT THE INCREASE OF QUALITY OF THE FINAL DESIGNS AND PRESENTATIONS.

FEEDBACK VIA COMMENTS

Leaving comment feedback via the 'share with teacher' feature is possible once a student turns in an assignment, but if students aren't ready to turn in a design and are seeking feedback there is another way to provide it. First, make sure you are added as an editor on the design, and then pop in and offer comments in the sidebar. Just highlight the text you want to comment on, click the quote bubble with the plus + on the right hand side, and leave feedback in the design. Students will receive notifications that a comment has been made, and they can go in and address the feedback accordingly.

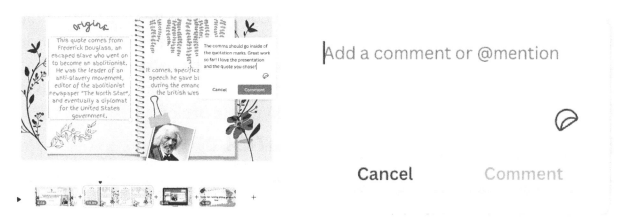

LEAVING VIDEO COMMENTS

Creating and dropping videos on student work is a fast and effective way to quickly give bird's eye view feedback; feedback that gives a quick overview to inform students if they are on the right track. This is especially important for research projects, science projects, presentations, design solutions, etc. As a literature and history teacher, I have also found video feedback is a fantastic way to assess writing. I will often read student work in the video and suggest revisions, grammar issues, and word choice. I would have loved this as an alternative to the sea of red ink I got in school! It is also a good strategy to differentiate for early learners or those who prefer multimodal forms of learning and communication. Written feedback can be cumbersome both on the teacher due to the time it can take, but also the student. Video killed the comment feedback star!

LEAVING AUDIO FEEDBACK WITH MOTE

Voice notes can be easily added to student designs by using the 'present and record' feature. When you get into the studio, simply turn your camera off and begin recording your audio feedback. This option is great for days you don't feel so camera ready! If you are me, that is probably everyday!

Another way to add audio to feedback is through Mote. Mote is a voice note google extension that can easily be added to Canva designs by downloading the extension, creating an account, and adding it to your extension toolbar. Click on the extension, record a voice message, then hit the share button to get the option of share link. The embed link is not currently supported, but if you copy the link and go to the 'embed' app that is integrated into Canva it will place the mote on the design. For work that will be printed, you can opt to add a QR code to the design!

EXIT TICKETS AND DIGITAL SCRATCH OFFS

Exit tickets are a great way to get informative feedback from your students with the goal of informing your instruction and assessing student comprehension of the day's lesson. There are a ton of exit ticket templates you can use if you search Canva, so I won't reinvent the wheel.

SCAN FOR DIGITAL SCRATCH OFF TICKET TEMPLATE

However, tickets are also a great way of rewarding students for hard work or for special occasions like birthdays, for reaching learning milestones, or just good behavior is part of building a positive classroom culture. Once you make a copy of the template you can customize the rewards based on what you have access to in your classroom. An in person classroom will have different incentives than that of an online classroom. Use this template to get started!

Destination Four: Getting the Most from *Canva* Apps

11

"TOGETHER, WE'RE UNLIMITED
TOGETHER WE'LL BE THE GREATEST
TEAM THERE'S EVER BEEN
GLINDA, DREAMS THE WAY WE PLANNED 'EM
IF WE WORK IN TANDEM"

— ELPHABA, WICKED BROADWAY MUSICAL

CANVA APP INTEGRATIONS AND APP SMASHING

CANVA INTERNAL INTEGRATION

Canva alone is an amazing platform where you can essentially design anything, but it also plays well with others! You know the lyrics…'It takes two to make a thing go right. It takes two to make it outta sight," by Rob Base and DJ EZ Rock, right? Well we are about to rock right now with app smashing and Canva! Canva has a plethora of built in apps that can enhance your designs with even more interactivity and help manage your workflow.

In the beginning of this book, I explained that Canva has replaced a lot of external tools that I used and consolidated them within the platform. While most are free, some are paid and may not work for your budget or school. For example, when it comes to apps that are integrated internally, Typeform may be an app used more by universities, while Pixton is free and can be easily and cost efficiently adopted by the K-12 environment. What I do know is that Canva is continuously adding apps and is dedicated to creating a platform that provides all sorts of educational solutions. Thumb your way to the next way to hitchhike your way through app smashing with Canva!

CANVA EXTERNAL APP INTEGRATION

Additionally, there are opportunities for app integrations where you can create templates in Canva and import them to other platforms. Canva has done a fantastic job of working with popular educational tools to ensure the platforms connect well. The most recent two are Flipgrid and Jamboard. You can find customizable templates specifically for these platforms. If you search Flipgrid backgrounds in the search tab you have a choice of 83 landscape templates and 50 portrait templates. This number is continuously growing.

Canva is also completely integrated and accessible in Book Creator. Book Creator is an app that allows teachers and students to build lessons, literature circles, units, etc in the form of interactive digital books. With Canva now integrated into their platform thousands of new images, videos, graphics and icons have been unlocked to make stunningly designed books. This is the app integration I am most excited about, and I have several units of how to use these two in your classroom in the template section!

CANVA NONINTEGRATED APP SMASHING

While internal and external integrations save time and streamline workflow, there are limitless possibilities to app smash outside of these conveniences. For example, there was a great blog that was released explaining how to app smash with Canva and Thinglink. Essentially, you are only limited to your imagination. For my recommended picks, descriptions of apps, and ideas on how you can app smash with Canva, keep reading. Hopefully, you will walk away with immediate ideas on how you can unlock creativity in your classroom and help students communicate their learning!

READ THE BLOG ON THINKGLINK + CANVA

CANVA INTERNAL APP INTEGRATION

Most of the Canva app integrations are developed by third parties, so in order to use them you must connect them to your account by either creating an account with the app (i.e. Bitmoji or Google Drive) and then logging into the app within Canva's platform. In order to find apps that are integrated with Canva, go to the menu on the left hand side of the dashboard and scroll down until you see 'more.' It should bring up a search bar that says 'search Canva apps.' You can search for specific apps to see if they are internally integrated, or select from the 'create something new,' or 'discover content from' section. You should also see options to import your media with a list of apps that are supported. You should DEFINITELY check this often to prevent missing a new update!

APP   DESCRIPTION

QR CODE BY CANVA

Canva has a QR generator built directly into the app! All you have to do is copy the link you want converted into a QR code, paste it into the box, and bam! A QR code is generated and pops up on your document! RIP QRgenerator.com. This eliminates the step of creating one externally and then importing it into the platform!

CLASSROOM APPLICATION

- QR Code Tutorial Videos
- QR Code Scavenger Hunt
- Flash Cards
- Remediation/Enrichment Centers
- Word Walls
- Embed Videos on Worksheets

- Check Answers/reflections
- Interactive Posters
- Embed Quiz Links in a Lesson
- About Me Activity
- QR Code Reading Stations
- QR Code Badges

APP

YOUTUBE

DESCRIPTION

With the Youtube app you can add YouTube content straight inside Canva and watch your favorite videos when you hit play. This is a fantastic way to enhance your lessons, activities, or student designed projects!

CLASSROOM APPLICATION

YOU CAN EMBED:

- Flipped Instruction
- Video Instructions
- Video Hook
- Explain a Lesson
- Sub Plans

- Science Lab
- Misconception Video
- Read a Book
- Math Problem Demo
- Start a Discussion or Debate

APP

BITMOJI

DESCRIPTION

The Bitmoji app nicely integrates into Canva so you can add your customized avatar to all of your designs. Open the Bitmoji app, search for a pose, click on it and resize it in your design!

CLASSROOM APPLICATION

- Bitmoji Classroom
- Give Feedback w/ Your Avatar!
- Make classroom rules!
- About the teacher video
- Bitmoji Comics
- Vocabulary

- Bitmoji Open House
- Bitmoji Posters and Anchor Charts
- Virtual Field Trip
- Interactive Bitmoji Library
- Bitmoji Escape Rooms

APP

PIXTON

DESCRIPTION

Pixton brings expressive characters to add to your designs. You can explain ideas and have students create diverse comics all within the Canva platform. High quality vector graphics with a variety of outfits, poses, hairstyles and colors.

SCAN FOR MORE IDEAS FROM PIXTON

CLASSROOM APPLICATION

- Comic Reading Log
- Math comic
- Historical Characters
- Culture Comic
- Indigenous Groups Comic
- Super Summarizer!

- Teach Dialogue Tags
- About Me Comic
- Plot Comic
- About Me Activity
- Word Detectives
- QR Code Badges

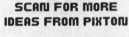

APP

CHARACTER BUILDER

DESCRIPTION

Character builder is much like Pixton, but with a limited number of combinations to create simple characters. You can customize their hair, skin tone, body, and facial expression.

CLASSROOM APPLICATION

- Create Classroom Posters
- Create Graphics
- Have Students Create Stories
- Create Custom Seat Tags for Students
- Student Avatars

APP

DRAW

DESCRIPTION

Canva draw app gives teachers and students the opportunity to do freehand drawing in the app! There are four drawing tools: pen, marker, highlight and glow pen. After the drawing is complete it can be resized, moved, and rotated. This feature can even be used with a Wacom tablet, but a finger, trackpad, or mouse will suffice!

SCAN FOR A VIDEO DEMO OF THE WACCOM TABLET BY STACY ROSHAN!

CLASSROOM APPLICATION

- Math Problems
- Diagramming Tool
- Graphic Organizers
- Graphing Problems
- Labeling
- Parts of Speech

- Stopmotion Animation
- Sketchnoting

SCAN ME

APP

GIPHY

DESCRIPTION

With Giphy integration you have access to the world's largest library of animated GIFs, now in Canva. Just add Giphy to your apps, and search for gifs by topic. Once you find one, just drag and drop! Try searching 'math gifs' and 'writing prompts' to get inspired!

CLASSROOM APPLICATION

- Animated Vocabulary
- Discussion Prompts
- Math Concepts
- Science Concepts
- Gif Story Telling
- Bellringers

- Content Memes
- SEL
- Exit Tickets

APP

EMBED

DESCRIPTION

With the embed app you can add virtually anything to your Canva designs; music, videos, media. I especially love the option to add music! I You can also embed all your favorite edtech tools to create hyperdocs and centralize all your unit materials in one place: your Canva design!

CLASSROOM APPLICATION

- Edpuzzle Videos
- Book Creator Books
- Google Forms
- Charts to Analyze
- Google Slides
- Ebooks/Flipbooks

- Poplets
- Wakelets
- Podcasts
- Padlets
- Nearpod Presentations

- Buncee
- Genially
- Desmos
- Songs

APP

GOOGLE APPS

DESCRIPTION

I'm going to lump all the Google Apps here... Canva integrates with Google Drive and Google photos making it super easy to access your files and drop them into your design. Google Maps are also available and can make for some interesting designs or lessons! I'm thinking a Zombie Apocalypse survival plan with the draw feature!

CLASSROOM APPLICATION

- Import Google Slides and Documents
- Create a Custom Map and Import
- Geography Unit: Modern World vs Ancient
- Recreate Historical Tours

APP

PUBLUU

DESCRIPTION

With Publuu you can create amazing flipbooks of your designs! This app requires an account and it has a freemium and paid version. If you leave a review of the app you will get a few months for free in exchange! You can also embed audio, links, videos, and text inside of the flipbook. This app is found by clicking the three dots in the Canva dashboard next to the download button. You can also search for it in the search bar.

CLASSROOM APPLICATION

- Unit Plans
- Interactive Text Books
- Professional Development
- Publish Student Journals
- Informational Texts

APP

TYPEFORM

DESCRIPTION

Typeform is a polling app that allows you to build in quizzes, polls, and surveys. You may prefer to just embed a Google Doc if you are K-12 , but Higher Ed may prefer this tool. It does cost money. You can also update the look of your Typeform by adding a custom-designed background made with Canva. You can connect it to a Google spreadsheet.

CLASSROOM APPLICATION

- Student-led Research
- Choose Your Own Adventure Stories
- Logical Thinking Problems
- Personality Tests
- Learning Styles Survey

- Publish Student Journals

APP   DESCRIPTION

EMOJI

The emoji app gives you access to thousands of expressions to add to your designs. Scan the QR code to get a copy of an emoji exit ticket that was in Canva!

SCAN FOR AN EMOJI EXIT TICKET TEMPLATE

CLASSROOM APPLICATION

- Emoji Feedback
- Climate Surveys
- Exit Tickets
- Emojiglyphics

- Emoji Check-in
- Mindfulness
- Progress Reports
- Emoji Poetry
- Censoring Student Faces

SCAN ME

APP   DESCRIPTION

PIXABAY

As if Canva didn't have a huge enough library already, you also have the power of free images from Pixabay. Add this app to gain access to over a million more photos to add to your designs.

CLASSROOM APPLICATION

- Projects
- Website Design
- Pamphlets and Brochures
- Student Assignments
- Lectures/instruction

CANVA EXTERNAL APP INTEGRATION

The power of Canva seamlessly integrates in a variety of platforms that you may already be using! It seems every month another educational tool or platform enables Canva integration, so continue to check back to see if any new tools have been added. Most of these external applications require registration, and in some cases a paid account, but if you already have access you are in for a treat! Below I will cover some of the most powerful integrations, a description of the platform, and examples of how you can leverage Canva for even more powerful learning experiences for students.

APP

BOOK CREATOR

DESCRIPTION

If you aren't familiar with Book Creator, it is a tool where teachers and students can create digital books to demonstrate or deliver learning experiences. The website does a fantastic job at sharing book templates and ideas with the educator community to help with getting started. By adding Canva, they supercharged the ability to create stunning book covers and pages right inside of the Book Creator! You simply click on the + sign when you are creating a book, then click on 'more.' Click on the 'Canva app' and you are ready to begin designing! When your design is finished you simply drop it into your book.

CLASSROOM APPLICATION

- Interactive Stories
- Digital Portfolios
- Project Based Learning Plans

- Science Reports
- Instructional Manuals
- Poetry Books

Food Saga Lesson

Creating a STEM Podcast

APP

PEARDECK

DESCRIPTION

Peardeck is a research aligned tool to provide educators a platform to deliver daily instruction, assess student learning, and improve learning outcomes for students. Recently, Canva was directly integrated into their platform with access to a series of ready-to-use, editable templates designed specifically with Pear Deck in mind! You can access these templates by scanning the QR code below. To use the slides, simply edit in Canva, or you can open as is in Google Slides or PowerPoint Online. Make sure you have installed the Pear Deck add-on. You then can add Pear Deck interactive elements, and present! You can also create your own from starting with a blank design and add them as the background to your slides.

CLASSROOM APPLICATION

- About Me
- Social Emotional Learning
- Science
- Social Studies

SCAN FOR ACCESS TO
PEARDECK TEMPLATES

Step 1: Create a Pear Deck account and add the extension to Google Slides or Power Point.

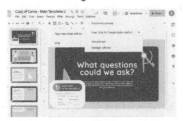

Step 2: Find a. template and make a copy.

Step 3: Edit slides and add Pear Deck Interactive elements!

Step 4: Publish and Present!

APP

FLIPGRID

DESCRIPTION

Flipgrid gets the power of student voice, and with the partnership with Canva, students and teachers have even more options to get creative when making videos. If you search Canva for 'Flipgrid' it will return a variety of templates that fit the dimensions for Flipgrid backgrounds. You can filter your search results by grade level, topic, and style. Simply download your design and upload to Flipgrid. You can even use Canva to create stickers for your Flipgrid videos. Simply create a design using graphics from the elements tab, and then download the file as a PNG file. You can use the background remover feature in Canva as well to create PNG stickers from images! The best part is getting students creating! Have them share their designs and create a video sharing what they learned!

CLASSROOM APPLICATION

- Stickers
- Backdrops
- Book Talks
- Create Frames
- About Me
- Mind Maps
- Virtual Postcards
- News Broadcast
- Graphic Organizers

SCAN ME

SCAN FOR A HITCHHIKER'S GUIDE FOR EDUCATORS BACKGROUND! CREATE A VIDEO SHARING HOW USE FLIPGRID+CANVA

INSTRUCTIONS

1. Login to Canva

2. In Canva, type "Flipgrid" in the template search bar. There over 100 backgrounds to choose from, or you can make your own from scratch!

3. Explore, copy, and customize your template. Click "Share" on the top right corner and download your design as a JPG.

4. Next, login to Flipgrid.

5. Click "Add a Backdrop" to import your Canva background or frame! Record a video!

APP

WIZER

wizer.me

DESCRIPTION

Wizer is a platform teachers use to create easy and fun interactive, digital worksheets. Now with the Canva integration it is easy to create beautiful interactive graphic organizers and worksheets that are automatically graded within the Wizer platform! What? Yes. You simply go to the Wizer website, login, and select 'create worksheet.' Next, you select 'import Canva design' and Canva will open up. You can select from one of the 36 templates, use as is, customize it, or create your own! Hit 'publish' and then it will take you back to Wizer. You can add multiple choice, fill in the blank, draw, short answer, or any of the other options! While Wizer does have a freemium, you can upgrade for $35.99 for the whole year!

CLASSROOM APPLICATION

- Science Diagrams
- Worksheet Headers
- Self Reflection
- Peer Reviews
- Math factors
- Story Elements
- Book Reviews
- Figurative language
- Parts of Speech
- Summarizing
- Geography
- Food Web
- Life Cycles
- Citing Evidence

SCAN ME

SCAN THE QR CODE FOR MORE INFORMATION ON WIZER

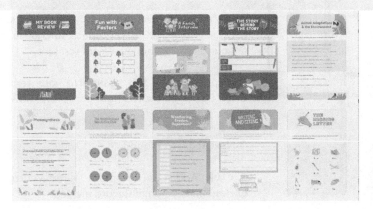

APP

SMARTPRESS

DESCRIPTION

If you haven't heard of Smartpress, they are a US based printing company. Smartpress and Canva have recently joined forces to provide a printing solution meaning educators and schools can now design their own projects on the Smartpress website. The online design option is available wherever you see the Canva logo alongside a Smartpress product. This is great for schools that want to design custom calendars, agendas, handwriting books, and other consumables that are traditionally used in the classroom. Check out some of my Smartpress templates!

CLASSROOM APPLICATION

- Flash Cards
- Calendars
- Student Agendas
- Bookmarks
- Certificates
- Stickers/Badges

- Welcome Postcards
- Classroom Posters
- Handwriting Journals
- Student Work Books
- Side Walk Signs

SCAN FOR IDEAS FOR WHAT TO PRINT FOR YOUR SCHOOL!

Design and print a welcome postcard to students prior to the first day of school!

Dear Parents and Students,

The Junior High Faculty Team (and our bitmojis) are excited to welcome all 7th and 8th grade students back for the 2020-2021 school year! Though the last 6 months has been filled with adversity, the new year brings anticipation of new beginnings, new technologies, and new friendships! We look forward to both classes maturing into great student leaders, helpers, and role models for our younger students.

We have been working hard to enhance our strong academic program with synchronous instruction for in-person and at-home (NTI) students. We look forward to a year of many blessings, and we trust the Holy Trinity will continue to guide our efforts.

In the meantime, scan the QR code below to view a meet the teacher playlist! We can't wait to see you all soon-- in person, or via Zoom!

Peace to all, and Go, Eagles!

Your Jr. High Team

Scan me

APP

WONDEROPOLIS

DESCRIPTION

Canva and Wonderopolis have now partnered! If you search for 'wonderopolis' there are WONDERFUL templates that you can use to help capture student learning! So far there are posters, postcards, comics, and other fantastic graphic organizers to pair with the 'wonder of the day' and other provoking questions about the world!

CLASSROOM APPLICATION

- Posters
- KWL charts
- Comic Strips
- Infographics
- Venn diagrams

- Brain maps
- Fun facts
- Interviews
- Pros and Cons

SCAN THE QR CODE TO CHECK OUT A POSTER TEMPLATE!

Search 'wonderopolis' in the template search bar to pull up close to 40 different templates you can pair with the 'wonder of the day.'

CANVA NON-INTEGRATED APPS APP SMASHING!

If you aren't familiar with the term App Smashing, it is a term coined by history teacher Greg Kulowiec and is defined as "the process of using multiple apps in conjunction with one another to complete a final task or project." App Smashing with Canva can provide you and your students with new creative ways to showcase learning. While the apps below aren't integrated with Canva (at least not yet), I'm going to share strategies and ideas on how to combine other apps to work in tandem with the Canva platform.

CANVA + MOTE

Mote is a voice memo tool and add-on that you create audio notes that save to your Google Drive! In order to embed a mote in a Canva design, all you have to do is get the link, add it to the QR code generator in Canva and tada! You have embedded a voice note! Why would you want to do this? If you are printing out your worksheets students can scan the QR code to have instructions read to them. Another novel use for app smashing with mote is student certificates with voice feedback or praise! You can also create an scannable word walls with voice, or flash cards where students can check for understanding. Bring energy and emotion to your Canva designs with the human voice! Check out this awesome example from Alex Isaacs.

SCAN THE QR CODE TO GET THE TEMPLATE

SCAN ME

CANVA + JAMBOARD

Similar to Flipgrid, you can also find Jamboard templates in Canva. If you search you will find 95 ready to use templates in all subject areas! Create awesome exit tickets, brainstorm templates, grammar Jamboards, graphic organizers, and even Battleship! I used this with my students during virtual learning for our Food Saga unit (mentioned in Book Creator section). Students brainstormed what food they were going to anthropomorphize and turn into a story and gave an elevator pitch for their plot. Other students provided sticky note feedback. I also used it as a substitution for a Gallery Walk for our gothic literature unit. Students posted their one pager designs in a Jamboard and gave feedback to peers virtually!

SCAN TO ACCESS THE COLLABORATIVE JAM BOARD!

SCAN ME

CANVA + WAKELET

Wakelet is a fantastic curation tool. You can jazz up your headers and graphics by creating them in Canva! Also, if you use Canva for classroom newsletters Wakelet is a great tool to curate them and share one link with parents. Not only do they have access to the current newsletter, but all the newsletters from the past as well. You can also use Wakelet to curate student work! If you are a teacher that has to turn in lesson plans, you can create a lesson template in Canva and then add each week to the Wakelet and share one link with your admin! Scan the code below to check out one pagers, students created in Canva and their Cospaces projects!

CANVA + GOOGLE SLIDES

This may seem like a no brainer, but you can design your slide decks in Canva and save them as the background! This also works with Powerpoint, or any presentation software. Want to take it to the next level? Use it with Nearpod or Pear Deck to create interactive lessons to assess learning while you present! I have used Canva + Google Slides for vocabulary units and included graphic organizers for analyzing words beyond the definition. Frayer Models, denotation/connotation activities, and even made student digital notebooks and literature circles prettier. Scan the QR below to check out the Hamilton Themed Student Notebook!

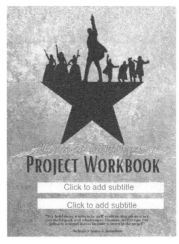

CANVA + CLASSDOJO

If you are a Classdojo user you know gamification and badges are all the rage! Use Canva to create custom badges students can earn in your classroom. You can search 'badges' in the search bar, customize the badge, download the file as a PNG, and upload it into ClassDojo! You can also design flyers, newsletters, and even back to school wish lists and post them. Check out how Mary Godoy is using these tools together in her classroom!

Mary Godoy
@MgodoyCorner

I just love @**canva** I created my back to school shopping list and posted it on @**ClassDojo**. My parents can start shopping sooner! #canvacreations

CANVA + SEESAW

Again, educators spoke. Canva listened. You can search for Seesaw templates within Canva! While there are only a few at the moment, the list is growing daily. They have a variety of templates to fit your Seesaw classroom needs. Check out the Scavenger Hunt created by Meagan de Silva!

Meagan da Silva @MeagDS · 8/9/18
A3. I made this hunt to encourage new and returning students to explore our campus. I'll add it to my activity library and students will post group selfies of themselves on @Seesaw #seesawchat @canva

CANVA + EDPUZZLE

With the embed app integrated into Canva it makes it super easy to add Edpuzzle videos to your designs! You can add them to provide background information on a lesson, add video of science experiments and then have students write about what they observed, or even videos of read alouds and have them practice literature skills like identifying, plot, theme, and figurative language! The possibilities are endless! Check out the template to the left, where I embedded EdPuzzle videos on Westward Expansion to help students learn the history they needed to know to create a video game on Manifest Destiny in Bloxels!

CANVA + EYEJACK

Eyejack is an augmented reality platform that allows you to add AR to almost anything. Including Canva designs! Whether you are creating AR flashcards, posters, instructions, or comic books, bringing your designs to life will surely engage students beyond the design. You can even create video presentations, and animations within Canva, download, then upload them to the Eyejack app along with a trigger image (your design).

Heather Brown
@browniesedbites

How awesome is this!?!? I love @canva for being a great starting block for creativity, but @eyejackapp helped me take it to the next level in under 2 minutes FOR FREE! Thanks to @JaimeDonally for sparking this idea!

#arvrinedu
#edutwitter
#edtech

CANVA + NATURAL READER TEXT TO SPEECH

Did you know that you and your students can add this Google Chrome extension to your Google Chrome browser and it works in Canva? This is great for littles, ESL students, or struggling readers! All they have to do is download it and pin it to their browser and highlight the text they want read to them. A headphone icon will appear. When they click on it it will open an audio control box and read the text to students. They can pause, rewind, and even translate text into other languages.

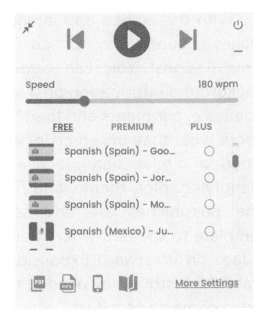

CANVA + QUIVER VISION

Want to bring more augmented reality action to your students? QuiverVision is using Canva to create augmented reality handwriting workbooks! Students color augmented reality coloring pages to learn about animal facts and then move on to perfect their handwriting with printable pages. Look for more AR enhanced consumables like writing journals and science notebooks to come out in the future. You can buy them for class, school, or district by going to QuiverVision.com.

CANVA + GENIALLY

Genially and Canva are great tools on their own, but with their powers combined you have uber interactive content that takes your lessons to another level! I have personally embedded Genially interactive images in my Canva Breakouts, but you can also embed presentations and quizzes directly into your Canva template! This is great for creating hyperdocs or simply adding a Genially to a Canva choice board! Want to add interactive maps to a history template with questions? Go for it! Want to embed an end of novel choice board? Boom! This is App smashing at it's finest!

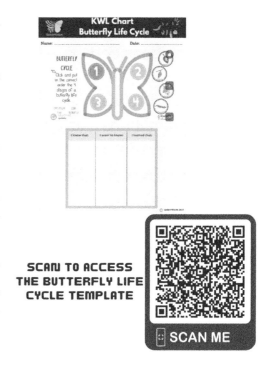

SCAN TO ACCESS THE BUTTERFLY LIFE CYCLE TEMPLATE

CANVA + CLASSROOMSCREEN

Classroomscreen.com is an online tool that allows you to engage students with 13 different widgets in your lesson. You can App Smash with Canva by adding QR codes to the templates for students to scan, adding media to your screen or gamifying your content! If you have a digital touch screen (like a clever touch), Canva adds the perfect aesthetic! In the Pi day lesson to the right the teacher uses the dice feature to roll to the first ten digits of Pi. It could be teacher against class, or individual students can come up and try! The possibilities are limitless!

SCAN TO WATCH A VIDEO ON CANVA AND CLASSROOMSCREEN. COM

CANVA + PARLAY

Parlayideas.com is a platform that makes it easy for teachers to facilitate, measure, and assess socratic discussions and conversations around educational topics in person and online. With Canva templates you can embed graphic organizers and collect learning artifacts beyond the conversation by embedding hyperlinks. Canva is also a great tool to create appealing visual covers like the one to the right. Sign up for Parlayideas.com and search community templates for my lesson on the industrial revolution with the driving question: Is Greed Fair?

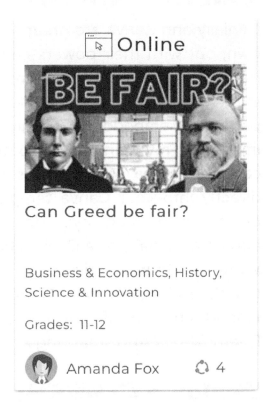

Online

Can Greed be fair?

Business & Economics, History, Science & Innovation

Grades: 11-12

Amanda Fox   4

CANVA + ALLSIDES

Another great tool to get meaningful conversations going is Allsidesforschool.org. When we get into topics like media bias and news literacy they have amazing activities that encourage students to participate in democracy through critical thinking and dialogue. The site has lesson plans and materials you can embed into your Canva templates to promote structured discussions and help students appreciate multiple perspectives.

CANVA + DESMOS

All right! Where are my math peeps at? You can embed Desmos lessons in Canva using the embed function! While the activities can not be done directly in Canva, this is a great opportunity to create a Math lesson, hyperdoc, or choice board for students! Using the hyperdoc template in the student templates section you simply find the lesson or lessons you want students to complete, copy the link, click on the 'embed' app in the left column of your dashboard, and bam! You have app smashed with Desmos and Canva. Good practice is to include an instructional video to introduce the math skill or concept. You ca use videos from Khan Academy and link or embed them directly in the document as well.

CANVA + SYMBALOO + STUDENT PORFOLIOS

Symbaloo is a cloud-based site that allows users to organize and categorize web links in the form of buttons. It works from a web browser allowing users to create a personalized virtual desktop! When students create portfolios in Canva it can be difficult to access them and grade them. I like to have students fill out a Google Form providing the edit link to their portfolios and save them to a Symbaloo. This makes it super easy to curate all student portfolios or notebooks in one place! I also color code my classes, so it's easy to visually scan and find each group!

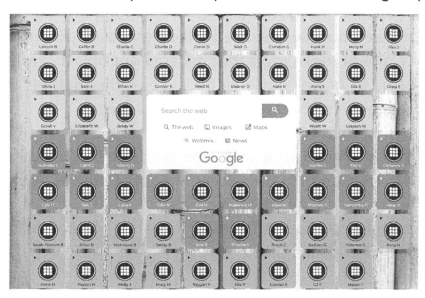

MADE IN *Canva*

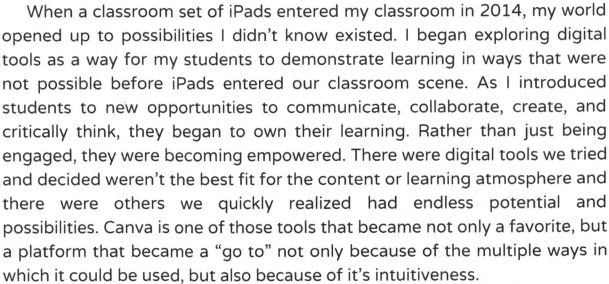

CANVA DRAW AND SKETCHNOTING

BY TISHA RICHMOND

When a classroom set of iPads entered my classroom in 2014, my world opened up to possibilities I didn't know existed. I began exploring digital tools as a way for my students to demonstrate learning in ways that were not possible before iPads entered our classroom scene. As I introduced students to new opportunities to communicate, collaborate, create, and critically think, they began to own their learning. Rather than just being engaged, they were becoming empowered. There were digital tools we tried and decided weren't the best fit for the content or learning atmosphere and there were others we quickly realized had endless potential and possibilities. Canva is one of those tools that became not only a favorite, but a platform that became a "go to" not only because of the multiple ways in which it could be used, but also because of it's intuitiveness.

Since I was first introduced to Canva, the platform has continued to evolve and respond to the needs of educators. Endless features, expanding partnerships with other incredible tools like Flipgrid, Pear Deck and Book Creator, and an intuitive and thoughtful design that is not only is easy to use, but also makes you look like a pro.

Quite honestly, I use Canva just as much, if not more, than I use Google, it's that critical to my daily productivity and creativity. As an instructional specialist I use Canva for all of my social media graphics and post scheduling, newsletters, presentation slides and video recordings, graphics of any sort, sketchnoting learning from books & PD sessions, badge & game card creation, and collaborative PD activities. Just when I think Canva can't get any better, I find another hidden gem that I didn't realize was there.

In my role as an instructional specialist, I have the joy of collaborating with teachers of all content areas and grade levels. The beautiful thing about Canva is it allows for students to express themselves creatively no matter their age or content being learned. Comic strips, infographics, videos, brochures, collaborative projects, sketchnoting, mind maps, book covers, flash cards, game boards, logos, design thinking, websites, portfolios, are just a few of the ways that students can demonstrate what they know. When we provide students with tools that allow them to create and share, we are opening up their world to endless possibilities.

DOODLING GAMES USING DRAW FEATURE

Just when I thought I couldn't love Canva anymore, they released the Draw feature and changed my world. This incredible feature allows you to draw in Canva using 4 different brushes: Pen, Marker, Glow Pen, and Highlighter. Within the Draw menu, the size, color, and transparency of each brush stroke can be changed allowing for fine detail, broad strokes, or shading. The ability to draw in sections and then move around or resize, creates a perfect canvas for Sketchnoting notes, design thinking, or collaborating. Couple Canva's doodle capabilities with all of the other incredible elements and features available in the platform, and you unlock infinite opportunities for student learning.

Sketchnoting is a powerful form of visual notetaking that has greatly benefited my students, as well as myself. Doodle games are a fantastic way to get students acquainted with skechnoting, explore the Canva Draw feature, and get their creative juices flowing. The following Canva doodle games are adapted from a pen and paper variation I learned from author of Doodle Revolution, Sunni Brown.

FACE IT

Original idea from Doodle Revolution, by Sunni Brown

1. Create an 11 x 8.5" design and duplicate the pages so every student has one.
2. Share the link in "edit" form so everyone will collaborate in the same design.
3. Have every student claim a page and open up the Draw feature under the "more" menu.
4. When you are ready, have students poise their stylus, or finger, over their page. When you say go, they make a haphazard wild mark on their page with at least one change of direction in it. Once the mark is drawn, they open their eyes and make a face from it; eyes, mouth, and nose.
5. After a minute is up, "present" the design on the screen to show all of the doodles.

This is a great way to get the room relaxed and bring a smile to everyone's face.

GRAPHIC JAM

Idea from Doodle Revolution, by Sunni Brown

For this game, students are given 20 seconds to doodle a word that you display on the screen. Often, I will start with more concrete words like coffee and apple and end with more abstract words like idea or brave.

1. Create an 11" x 8.5" design that includes 1 blank page for each student.
2. Have every student claim a page.
3. Share out a word with the class. Using the "Draw" feature in Canva, students draw their doodle on their claimed page. After the 20 seconds is up, "present" the design on the screen to show all of the doodles.
4. Have students erase and then repeat with a new word.

I love this activity because it helps students visualize the images in their head. It also shows that everyone visualizes things differently. There is no right or wrong way to doodle an image. The important part is that it represents something to the person who is doodling it.

MORE SKETCHNOTE TEMPLATES

Destination Five: Answers to Templates that Rocket Student Engagement

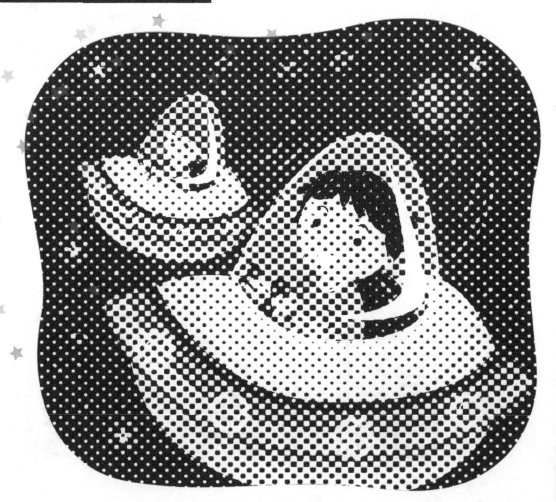

> **"SO ONCE YOU DO KNOW WHAT THE QUESTION ACTUALLY IS, YOU'LL KNOW WHAT THE ANSWER MEANS."**
>
> **— DOUGLAS ADAMS**

TEMPLATES TO ROCKET STUDENT ENGAGEMENT

CANVA TEMPLATES

The power of remixable templates is undeniable in the education galaxy. As teachers we are always looking for ways to save time, without sacrificing quality, content, or level of engagement. That's how TeachersPayTeachers has built an empire off of educators selling their best work. In this section I am providing turn key lessons that I have created as a result of tried and true classroom use. The goal is that you can truly see the power of Canva and you leave this book inspired to remix, reuse, and create your own lessons. I hope this section in the book becomes dogeared and revisited, and that you share anything you create with our educator community on Facebook, #TheCanvaClassroom.

CANVA TEMPLATES

This section is organized by topics/content area as best as I could. Each lesson starts with a title, description, learning goals, and teaching tips. The gray side bar for each lesson includes information that is often needed in lesson planning: standards, essential questions, the type of activity it is (individual, group, collaborative, etc) and any apps needed to successfully execute the lesson. I have additionally worked with Erik Francis to ensure each lesson is aligned to a DOK level. Remember, DOK levels are the expected experience that students will gain from the lesson. It is the desired outcome, but won't necessarily always be the case. You can always alter the templates to go up and down a level to suit your learning objectives! I have also included a QR code at the bottom of each page that will take you to the template link of the design to ensure you have access to it in your personal Canva dashboard.

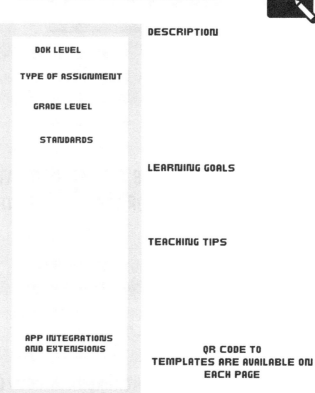

GRAPHIC ORGANIZERS

DESCRIPTION

DOK LEVEL

TYPE OF ASSIGNMENT

GRADE LEVEL

STANDARDS

BLANK TEMPLATE EXAMPLE

LEARNING GOALS

TEACHING TIPS

APP INTEGRATIONS AND EXTENSIONS

QR CODE TO TEMPLATES ARE AVAILABLE ON EACH PAGE

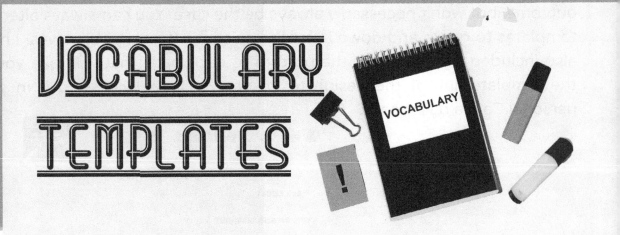

VOCABULARY TEMPLATES

TO ACCESS ALL THE TEMPLATES IN THIS SECTION
SCAN THE QR CODE OR GO TO THE WEBSITE BELOW.

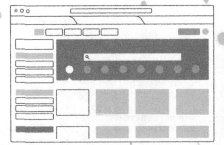

SCAN ME

WWW.TEACHERGOALS.COM/CANVATEMPLATES

STRANGER WORD MATRIX

DOK LEVEL (2)

TYPE OF ASSIGNMENT

Individual/Demonstration

GRADE LEVEL

3-12

STANDARDS

CCSS.ELA-LITERACY.L.3.2.E
Use conventional spelling for high-frequency and other studied words and for adding suffixes to base words (e.g., sitting, smiled, cries, happiness).

ESSENTIAL QUESTIONS

- How can the meaning of words be interpreted technically?
- What impact could morphology and grammatical units have on the overall meaning of a word?
- How can you use morphology to decode language?

APP INTEGRATIONS AND EXTENSIONS

 Canva

DESCRIPTION

With this template students are encouraged to explore morphology, prefixes, roots, and suffixes. Leveraging pop culture, I have created a Stranger Things themed video that explains what a morpheme is and how words can be broken down into their smallest grammatical unit. This takes students beyond just defining a word and helps develop decoding skills they can apply to unfamiliar words in the future.

LEARNING GOALS

- Students will become familiar with morphology.
- Students will break words down into smaller grammatical units.
- Students will create derivatives, or new words, by adding affixes to root words.

TEACHING TIPS

Before using the Stranger Word Matrix, make sure students are familiar with morphemes, prefixes, suffixes, and root words. You may want to do one as a whole group before assigning the template to indivudal students.

QR CODE TO TEMPLATE

Consider using this template to teach domain specific vocabulary outside of language arts and the English classroom. I have also used the template as a Flipgrid background and have had students make videos while communicating their understanding of language and semantics.

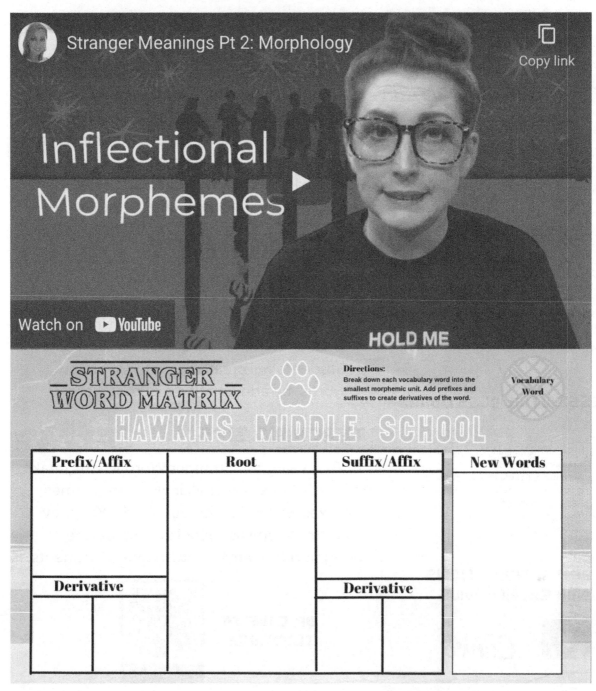

MIND FRAYER MODEL

DESCRIPTION

The Mind Frayer Model is another pop culture connection to my Stranger Vocabulary unit, putting a Stranger Things spin on a graphic organizer classic. You can assign this to students to help them gain a deeper understanding of vocabulary through engaging with the word in various ways. I like to use the Bitmoji browser extension and have them create an avatar for their word. You simple type the word, right click on the image you want and then copy it into your design. They then have to find a synonym, antonym, define the word, and visualize it with an image.

LEARNING GOALS

- Students will identify unfamiliar concepts and vocabulary.
- Students will create a visual reference for concepts and vocabulary.

TEACHING TIPS

You can assign this graphic organizer as a bell ringer and give them a new word each day. They can work individually or in pairs to complete this, and even add videos to their graphic or mote audio with the Mote extension explaining why they chose the visual representation they chose!

DOK LEVEL  2

TYPE OF ASSIGNMENT

Individual/Demonstration

GRADE LEVEL

3-12

STANDARDS

- CCSS.ELA-LITERACY.RF.
Know and apply grade-level phonics and word analysis skills in decoding words.
- CCSS.ELA-LITERACY.RF.
Use combined knowledge of all letter-sound correspondences, syllabication patterns, and morphology (e.g., roots and affixes) to read accurately unfamiliar multisyllabic words in context and out of context.

ESSENTIAL QUESTIONS

- How can the meaning of words be interpreted technically?
- How do I use synonyms, antonyms, and closely related words to understand the meaning of a word or phrase?
- How can I visualize words with multimedia elementss?

APP INTEGRATIONS AND EXTENSIONS

   mote

Canva

QR CODE TO TEMPLATE

Use chrome extensions and the integrated apps within Canva to make your graphic organizers media rich. This also gives students the opportunity to communicate what they know in multiple ways. I also like to provide the link to visuwords.com so students can interact with word relationships visually. If students are struggling to pronounce a word they can also use the Natural Reader Text to Speech extension.

BLANK TEMPLATE

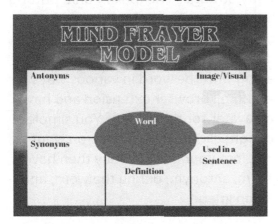

VISUWORD GRAPHIC

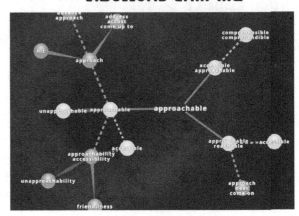

BITMOJI CHROME EXTENSION FOR CUSTOM WORDS!

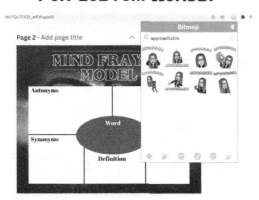

USING MOTE!

EXAMPLE OF A COMPLETED MIND FRAYER MODEL

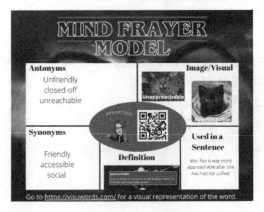

SHADES OF MEANING

DESCRIPTION

The Shades of Meaning graphic organizers offer students an opportunity to explore the denotation and connotation of words and how those nuances in language impact the meaning of a sentence or text. You can use the paint chip version of the activity to cover multiple vocabulary words, or have students continue with the Stranger Vocabulary theme, and use the Stranger Meanings version.

DOK LEVEL 3

TYPE OF ASSIGNMENT

Individual/Demonstration

GRADE LEVEL

6-12

STANDARDS

- CCSS.ELA-LITERACY.L.6.5
Demonstrate understanding of figurative language, word relationships, and nuances in word meanings.
- CCSS.ELA-LITERACY.L.6.5.C
Distinguish among the connotations (associations) of words with similar denotations (definitions) (e.g., stingy, scrimping, economical, unwasteful, thrifty).
- CCSS.ELA-LITERACY.L.6.6
Acquire and use accurately grade-appropriate general academic and domain-specific words and phrases; gather vocabulary knowledge when considering a word or phrase important to comprehension or expression.

LEARNING GOALS

- Students will explore denotative and connotative meanings.
- Students will discuss how word choice contributes to the tone of piece of writing.

ESSENTIAL QUESTIONS

- What is denotation?
- How do nuances in meaning impact the meaning of a sentence or text?
- How does word choice impact the author's tone or meaning of a text?

TEACHING TIPS

You can use vocabulary words that you have chosen, or have students pick their own from a novel or text. From there you can engage in discussions on how different words may have changed the author's tone altogether!

APP INTEGRATIONS AND EXTENSIONS

 Canva

QR CODE TO TEMPLATE

Consider using this to teach author's craft through word choice. You can provide sentences to students, or have them search for sentences in a text on their own. Students then replace the word with a synonym and explain how the substitution changes the tone of the sentence or text. Students can create a video explaining their thought process and add it to the document. I have included a link to a video demonstrating how I introduce denotation and connotation to students through the show Stranger Things. Scan the QR code to view the video!

QR CODE TO STRANGER MEANINGS VIDEO

WORDLE WALL

DESCRIPTION

Bring the pop culture phenomenon of Wordle to your classroom with the Wordle Wall Template. Students will use a Wordle website generator to create their own vocabulary based Wordles and share them to a Padlet for their peers to experience! Once they have created their Wordle they will complete a vocabulary activity to visualize the word, define it, and find words of similar meaning.

LEARNING GOALS

- Students will create a Wordle puzzle with your classroom vocabulary and add it to our class wall.
- Students will determine the meaning of unknown words.

TEACHING TIPS

Provide students with a list of words you are studying. For elementary this may be CVC words. This activity is fantastic for all content areas! You may want to assign each student a word ahead of time to prevent duplicates. Have students post the Wordles to a class Padlet, or you can create a physical Wordle Wall Calendar (like a Wordle of the day) add a QR code, and have them scan to figure out the word!

QR CODE TO TEMPLATE

DOK LEVEL (2)

TYPE OF ASSIGNMENT
Individual/Creation/Interactive

GRADE LEVEL
2-12

STANDARDS

- CCSS.ELA-LITERACY.CCRA.L.4 Determine or clarify the meaning of unknown and multiple-meaning words and phrases by using context clues, analyzing meaningful word parts, and consulting general and specialized reference materials, as appropriate.
- CCSS.ELA-LITERACY.L.6.6 Acquire and use accurately grade-appropriate general academic and domain-specific words and phrases; gather vocabulary knowledge when considering a word or phrase important to comprehension or expression.

ESSENTIAL QUESTIONS

- How can I increase my vocabulary?
- How does the understanding of vocabulary increase our comprehension of challenging texts?
- How do we determine the meaning of unknown words?

APP INTEGRATIONS AND EXTENSIONS

 *Canva*

padlet

Wordle can be used as a stand alone assignment or a daily exercise to increase a students vocabulary in order to aid in reading comprehension. Consider using it to teach foreign languages, domain specific vocabulary, site words, or words found in novels or storybooks.

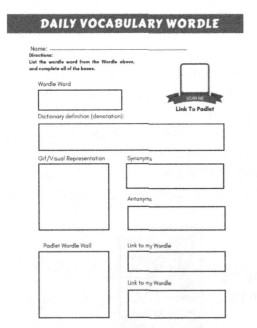

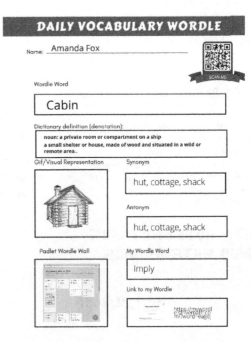

HEXAGONAL THINKING

DESCRIPTION

Hexagonal thinking is a a great tool to get students thinking about connecting ideas and concepts using key terms placed on hexagons. The activity is fantastic because given a classroom full of students no two designs, connections, or ways of thinking are going to end up the same. Using the drag and drop function, students will work alone or with a partner to drag the terms to the hexagons and connect or group ideas. They can color code the hexagons by grouping.

LEARNING GOALS

- Students will make connections between key terms and ideas.
- Students will present and defend their thinking through collaborative discussions.

TEACHING TIPS

Assign this to individuals, partners, or small groups to complete. You could develop this tool into a full fledged hyperdoc by adding define and explore activities prior to completing the hexagonal thinking activity. After the activity, have a class discussion where students defend their connections and way of thinking.

DOK LEVEL 3

TYPE OF ASSIGNMENT

Individual/Group/Interactive

GRADE LEVEL

K-12

STANDARDS

CCSS.ELA-LITERACY.SL.
Present information, findings, and supporting evidence such that listeners can follow the line of reasoning and the organization, development, and style are appropriate to task, purpose, and audience.

Make strategic use of digital media and visual displays of data to express information and enhance understanding of presentations.

CCSS.ELA-LITERACY.SL.
Engage effectively in a range of collaborative discussions (one-on-one, in groups, and teacher-led) with diverse partners on grade 6 topics, texts, and issues, building on others' ideas and expressing their own clearly.

ESSENTIAL QUESTIONS

- How can I make connections between key ideas and terms?
- How can I defend these connections to my teacher and classmates?

APP INTEGRATIONS AND EXTENSIONS

 Canva

QR CODE TO TEMPLATE

Hexagonal thinking can be used in many content areas and address a variety of standards. Below I have provided examples of a blank template. Additionally, I have provided an example from literature using key terms and ideas from The Outsiders and an example from social studies using types of government. I have also seen this done before in the science and art classrooms addressing chemical reactions, artistic styles and artists.

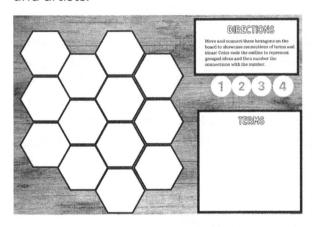

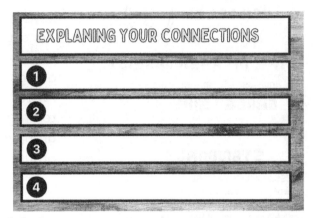

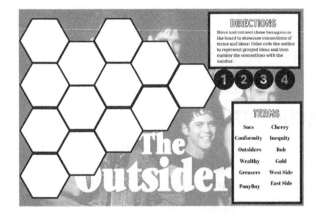

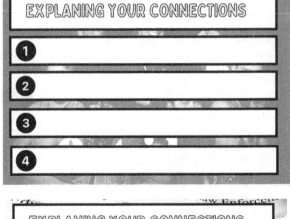

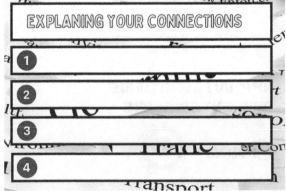

POETRY & LIT TEMPLATES

"VOGON POETRY IS OF COURSE, THE THIRD WORST IN THE UNIVERSE. THE SECOND WORST IS THAT OF THE AZGOTHS OF KRIA. DURING A RECITATION BY THEIR POET MASTER GRUNTHOS THE FLATULENT OF HIS POEM "ODE TO A SMALL LUMP OF GREEN PUTTY I FOUND IN MY ARMPIT ONE MIDSUMMER MORNING" FOUR OF HIS AUDIENCE DIED OF INTERNAL HAEMORRHAGING AND THE PRESIDENT OF THE MID-GALACTIC ARTS NOBBLING COUNCIL SURVIVED BY GNAWING ONE OF HIS OWN LEGS OFF. GRUNTHOS WAS REPORTED TO HAVE BEEN "DISAPPOINTED" BY THE POEM'S RECEPTION, AND WAS ABOUT TO EMBARK ON A READING OF HIS 12-BOOK EPIC ENTITLED "MY FAVOURITE BATHTIME GURGLES" WHEN HIS OWN MAJOR INTESTINE, IN A DESPERATE ATTEMPT TO SAVE HUMANITY, LEAPT STRAIGHT UP THROUGH HIS NECK AND THROTTLED HIS BRAIN.
THE VERY WORST POETRY OF ALL PERISHED ALONG WITH ITS CREATOR, PAUL NEIL MILNE JOHNSTONE OF REDBRIDGE, IN THE DESTRUCTION OF THE PLANET EARTH. VOGON POETRY IS MILD BY COMPARISON."

—THE HITCHHIKER'S GUIDE TO THE GALAXY, 1979, DOUGLAS ADAMS

TO ACCESS ALL THE TEMPLATES IN THIS SECTION SCAN THE QR CODE OR GO TO THE WEBSITE BELOW.

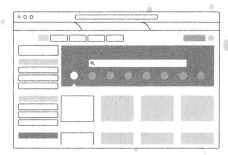

SCAN ME

WWW.TEACHERGOALS.COM/CANVATEMPLATES

MAGNETIC POETRY

DESCRIPTION

With the Canva drag and drop feature your students can easily create magnetic poems! You can create a list of words for students that fall under a particular theme, or you can have students pick their own words and curate their own collections. This is great for any age group. You can use it to teach parts of speech and group words under their function, or scale it up for older students to teach diction, mood, tone, and author's purpose.

LEARNING GOALS

- Students will create poems from a list of words paying attention to parts of speech.
- Students will create a thematic poem from the words given.
- Students will create a new collection of words based on a theme provided by the teacher.

TEACHING TIPS

I have included three templates for you in this collection. One is focused on elementary and grouped by parts of speech, another has students generate Shakespearian insults, and the next is about Vogon Poetry (THGTG Reference). You can change the background and customize the words to fit your learning goals and standards.

DOK LEVEL

TYPE OF ASSIGNMENT

Individual/Demonstration/Interactive

GRADE LEVEL

K-12

STANDARDS

- CCSS.ELA-LITERACY.RL.8.4
Determine the meaning of words and phrases as they are used in a text, including figurative and connotative meanings; analyze the impact of specific word choices on meaning and tone, including analogies or allusions to other texts.
- CCSS.ELA-LITERACY.RL.8.2
Determine a theme or central idea of a text and analyze its development over the course of the text, including its relationship to the characters, setting, and plot; provide an objective summary of the text.

ESSENTIAL QUESTIONS

- What is magnetic poetry?
- What is the relationship between tone and theme?
- How do words and phrases contribute to tone and meaning of a text?
- How can I use words to convey imagery and mood?

APP INTEGRATIONS AND EXTENSIONS

Canva

QR CODE TO TEMPLATE

SCAN ME

This lesson is so versatile! You can use this in science, history, literature, STEM, math...really any content area as long as they have a topic, theme, and the words to drag and drop. In honor of the book's theme I created a Vogon Poetry template so you can see how creative you can get with it (it's only the 3rd worse poetry in the universe)!

 With older students I tend to let them go rogue and create their own. A lot of times after I have assigned this lesson students will share a customized version they created. I love the creativity that it elicits from students and the desire to continue creating and applying this form of poetry in their personal lives.

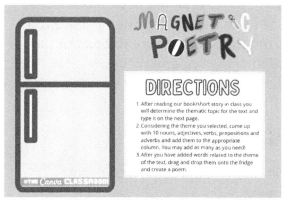

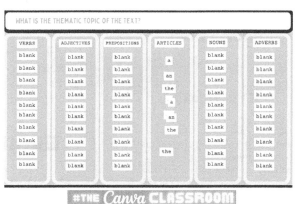

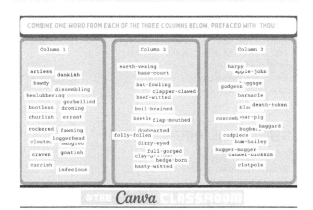

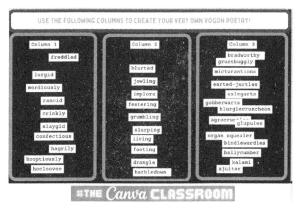

BLACK OUT POETRY

DOK LEVEL ③

TYPE OF ASSIGNMENT

Individual/Demonstration/Creation

GRADE LEVEL

4-12

STANDARDS

- CCSS.ELA-LITERACY.RL.8.4 Determine the meaning of words and phrases as they are used in a text, including figurative and connotative meanings; analyze the impact of specific word choices on meaning and tone, including analogies or allusions to other texts.
- CCSS.ELA-LITERACY.RL.8.2 Determine a theme or central idea of a text and analyze its development over the course of the text, including its relationship to the characters, setting, and plot; provide an objective summary of the text.

ESSENTIAL QUESTIONS

- What is blackout poetry?
- What is the relationship between tone and theme?
- How do words and phrases contribute to tone and meaning of a text?
- How can I use words to convey imagery and mood?

APP INTEGRATIONS AND EXTENSIONS

 Canva

DESCRIPTION

With the Canva draw feature your students can easily create their own black out poetry that centers around themes, motif, and diction in novels and short stories, or just for the sake of creating poetry. Pick a page from a story you are reading and add it to your template. Students skim the page for words that resonate, or tie to the theme. They will use the black marker from the draw feature to box out the words to create their own poetry piece!

LEARNING GOALS

- Students will examine the tone, mood, and theme of a text.
- Students will create a new work of similar theme using the black out poetry method.

TEACHING TIPS

I have included pages in the template for you to use from popular novels and short stories, but you can customize these to fit the texts you are covering in your classroom. I have also included examples to share with students. Encourage students to make a list of the words in the order they find them to devise a poem from the words in the text. The challenge is the new poem must have the same theme/mood as the original text

QR CODE TO TEMPLATE

When having students complete this activity you can choose to focus on diction, theme, mood, figurative language, denotation, or imagery. Just be sure that you have modeled the skill you are wanting reflected in your student's poetry and that you have communicated clear expectations of what you want to assess. You can also adapt this for littles or other content areas like history or science using articles!

LETTER 1

St. Petersburgh, Dec. 11th, 17—
To Mrs. Saville, England

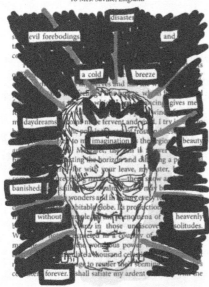

SCAN FOR VIDEO INSTRUCTIONS

THE MASKED SINGER

DOK LEVEL (4)

TYPE OF ASSIGNMENT

Individual or Group/Analysis Essay

GRADE LEVEL

2-12

STANDARDS

The standards for this template will vary depending on the content and grade level. Here are standards for the poetry unit.

- CCSS.ELA-LITERACY.CCRA.R.7
Integrate and evaluate content presented in diverse formats and media, including visually and quantitatively, as well as in words.

- CCSS.ELA-LITERACY.CCRA.R.8
Delineate and evaluate the argument and specific claims in a text, including the validity of the reasoning as well as the relevance and sufficiency of the evidence.

- CCSS.ELA-LITERACY.CCRA.R.9
Analyze how two or more texts address similar themes or topics in order to build knowledge or to compare the approaches the authors take.

ESSENTIAL QUESTIONS

- How is the author's tone reflected in his or her word choice? meaning within a text?
- How does point of view affect a story?
- How does the author use figurative language in the text?

APP INTEGRATIONS AND EXTENSIONS

DESCRIPTION

This fun themed template is a rift off the show "The Masked Singer." Students click on each masked singer and are taken to a page with an audio clue, two text clues, and a link to unmask the 'singer.' After students complete the activity they fill out a graphic organizer on each 'singer' and answer questions. This can be replicated for any content area! The Masked Poet is the example in the template, but you can use it for history, science, book characters...the possibilities are endless!

LEARNING GOALS

Learning goals will vary depending on content area. Here is an example for the poetry lesson:
- Students will explore poetry as a medium of written and spoken expression.
- Students will analyze poems for structure and author's craft citing specific examples.

TEACHING TIPS

You will need to provide the template link for students and ask them to view it present mode for the hyperlinks to work. If you share the view only link it will play as a video and won't work. The activity is a DOK 2, but you can increase the rigor of the activity by adding a higher level task at the end (ie: essay)

QR CODE TO TEMPLATE

Below, I have provided an example template using poets. Additionally, Michael Harvey, New Zealand educator, has adapted this template for the high school chemistry classroom using molecules. The additional template can be accessed below by scanning the QR code. I want to note to be careful with the hyperlinks in the template. This activity is a little complex. If you have any issues when adapting it to your content be sure to reach out!

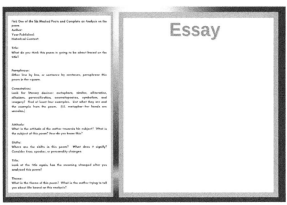

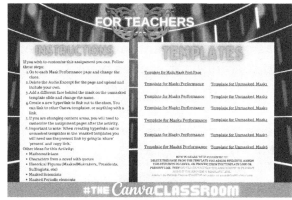

CANVA ONE PAGER

DESCRIPTION

Using Canva, students can create one pagers on a Gothic Literature short story. By using Canva teachers can eliminate hesitant artists by using the repository of graphic elements and images in the platform. Once posters are designed and printed, students will then use pens to handwrite textual evidence from the story to support the theme, characterization, author's craft, and figurative language used in the text.

LEARNING GOALS

- Students will create a multimedia representation of a short story.
- Students will analyze the author's craft.
- Students will provide textual evidence to support their images and design.

TEACHING TIPS

When assigning a one pager, you can have students address a short story, novel, or poem. I assigned different short stories within the Gothic Literature genre and had them work in groups to produce one pagers. Additionally, they had to create a virtual reality space that showcased the elements of the story and included biographical information about the author. The QR code below will give you access to the Bitmoji Classroom assignment that includes text selections. I had students start from a blank template and create the one pagers from scratch.

DOK LEVEL (4)

TYPE OF ASSIGNMENT
Individual/Group/Creation

GRADE LEVEL
3-12

STANDARDS

- CCSS.ELA-LITERACY.RL.
Determine a theme or central idea of a text and analyze its development over the course of the text, including its relationship to the characters, setting, and plot; provide an objective summary of the text.
- CCSS.ELA-LITERACY.RL.
Cite several pieces of textual evidence to support analysis of what the text says explicitly as well as inferences drawn from the text.
- CCSS.ELA-LITERACY.W.
Draw evidence from literary or informational texts to support analysis, reflection, and research.

ESSENTIAL QUESTIONS

- How is the author's tone reflected in his or her word choice? meaning within a text?
- What is the theme of the story?
- How can I craft a thematic statement?
- How does point of view affect a story?
- How does the author use figurative language in the text?
- How can I use images to convey the meaning of the story?

APP INTEGRATIONS AND EXTENSIONS

QR CODE TO GOTHIC LIT ASSIGNMENT

SCAN ME

Canva Assignment Requirements:

1. Include the author and title of the story.
2. A border which represents key themes from what you have read.
3. An image with a quotation woven into or around it that should in some way represent what you consider to be the most important symbol in the text.
4. Words and/or images that show the significance of the setting in some way.
5. Three or more important quotations from the texts that contribute to the theme.
6. Images and/or doodled words that represent the key characters from the text and perhaps how they've changed.
7. Images and quotations that show the author's style of writing, and the power of the language that is used.

When you are done designing your one pager use white, gold, and metallic pens to add evidence from the text to support your design and image choices.

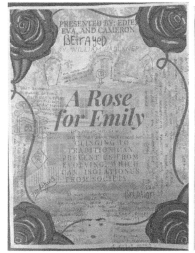

Cospaces Extension Activity Requirements for one pager:

QR CODE TO
VIRTUAL REALITY
ASSIGNMENT

QR CODE TO
THE YELLOW
WALLPAPER

QR CODE TO
THE CASK OF
AMONTILLADO

SOCIAL MEDIA TEMPLATES

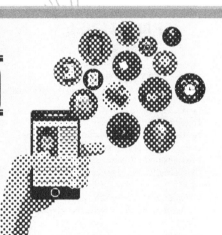

TO ACCESS ALL THE TEMPLATES IN THIS SECTION
SCAN THE QR CODE OR GO TO THE WEBSITE BELOW.

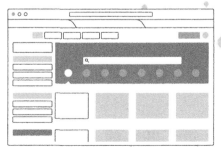 

WWW.TEACHERGOALS.COM/CANVATEMPLATES

INSTAGRAM TEMPLATE

DESCRIPTION

Using social media templates is a great way to have students showcase their learning! Most kids are familiar with social media, and this gives them a safe option to create a social media post without actually being on social media. In this Instagram template, students create an Instagram page for a fictional character addressing the the plot in the book, indirect and direct characterization, and theme! It can be adapted to any content area.

LEARNING GOALS

- Students will analyze the plot of a story and create images that correspond to the plot.
- Students will identify direct and indirect characterization and create an instagram post reflecting this.
- Students will determine the theme of a text.

TEACHING TIPS

Assign this to individuals, partners, or small groups to complete. Students will design an Instagram page for a fictional character following the prompts on each image. You can change these prompts to reflect your content area, or learning objective. This is also a great history activity!

DOK LEVEL 3

TYPE OF ASSIGNMENT
Individual/Group

GRADE LEVEL
3-12

STANDARDS

- CCSS.ELA-LITERACY.RL.
Determine a theme or central idea of a text and analyze its development over the course of the text, including its relationship to the characters, setting, and plot; provide an objective summary of the text.
- CCSS.ELA-LITERACY.RL.
Cite several pieces of textual evidence to support analysis of what the text says explicitly as well as inferences drawn from the text.

ESSENTIAL QUESTIONS

- How can I identify and visualize the plot elements of the text?
- How does the author use indirect and direct characterization in the text?
- What is the overall theme of the text?

APP INTEGRATIONS AND EXTENSIONS

Canva

QR CODE TO TEMPLATE

SCAN ME

The template below is made using a video presentation, so student work can be exported and showcased as an Instagram reel on a classroom Instagram page. You can also share student work through Seesaw or by generating view links and sending them to parents! You can create pages for historical figures, periodic elements, scientists, shapes, etc. The template can be easily adapted to include what ever skill you want students to demonstrate. For math you could have a Pythagoras page, and let students work out problems like they are the mathematician! In the next few pages I am including templates to other social media platforms for your use. You can use the same concept for each of the templates.

Create a post for a significant event that happened in the story complete with a caption explanation from the character's perspective.

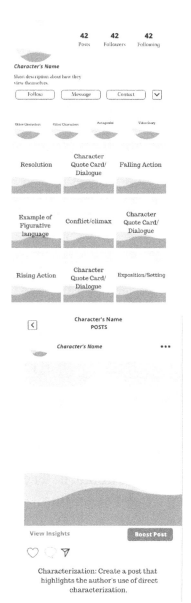

Characterization: Create a post that highlights the author's use of direct characterization.

Characterization: Create a post that highlights the author's use of indirect characterization.

AMAZON BOOK REVIEW

 Your Name
Verified Reader

 Book Name

Add a title/one line summary

Add a photo of your favorite page and a video explaining why you chose it.

SCAN ME

Add a written review. Include the genre, who the main character was, an overview of what it was about, and what you liked most about it. Try to write the review without giving away the ending!

QR CODE TO TEMPLATE

FACEBOOK TEMPLATE

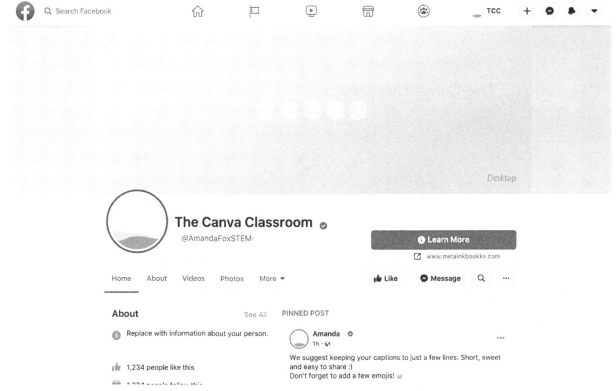

QR CODE TO TEMPLATE

PINTEREST TEMPLATE

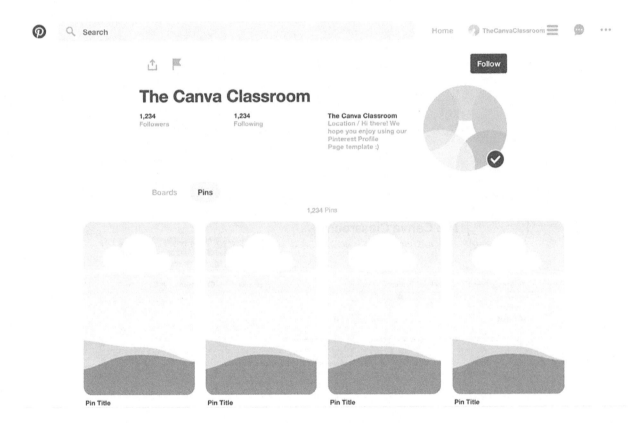

QR CODE TO TEMPLATE

SCAN ME

YOUTUBE TEMPLATE

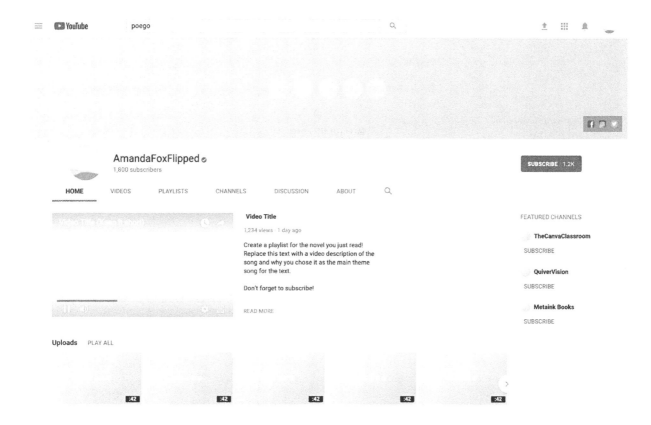

QR CODE TO TEMPLATE

TIK TOK TEMPLATE

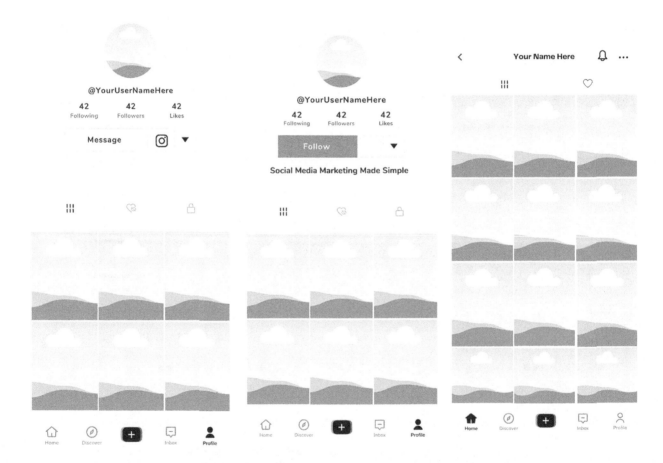

QR CODE TO TEMPLATE

SOCIAL CALENDAR TEMPLATE

Social Media Calendar

WEEK OF   MONTH/DAY - MONTH/DAY

Monday	Tuesday	Wednesday	Thursday	Friday	Saturday	Sunday
Topic	Topic	Topic	Topic	Topic	Topic	Topic
Caption	Caption	Caption	Caption	Caption	Caption	Caption

QR CODE TO TEMPLATE

SCAN ME

FAKE TEXT CONVERSATION

Tip: Another great option for fake texts between book characters of historical figures is the app @TextingStory where you can create a fake video and embed it in your Canva designs!

QR CODE TO TEMPLATE

SCAN ME

BOOK CREATOR UNITS

BOOK CREATOR

TO ACCESS ALL THE TEMPLATES IN THIS SECTION SCAN THE QR CODE OR GO TO THE WEBSITE BELOW.

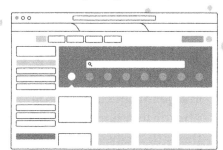

SCAN ME

WWW.TEACHERGOALS.COM/CANVATEMPLATES

FOOD SAGA UNIT

DESCRIPTION

English Language Arts Common Core standards are a perfect match for digital media projects. Each trimester the #foodsaga project focuses on introducing or assessing specific writing and language convention standards. With each new trimester the writing and language convention standards of focus will change.

Additionally, students use images to creatively sequence and craft a story. The problem or dilemma is: How can I tell a story through a sequence of edited photos that not only personify, but anthropomorphize food? As students venture through this creative process they will be prompted to think critically about elements of figurative language, writing narratives and author's craft, punctuation, puns, humor, and how to leverage digital tools to communicate.

LEARNING GOALS

- Students will master narrative storytelling through dialogue while addressing specific language conventions as outlined in the rubric, while paying attention to author's purpose.
- Students will will photograph their food (or use images from Canva), edit and arrange the photos in a narrative sequence, and publish them to a classroom bookshelf using Book Creator.

DOK LEVEL (4)

TYPE OF ASSIGNMENT

Individual/Creation/Writing

GRADE LEVEL

3-8

DURATION

3 Weeks

STANDARDS

- CCSS.ELA-LITERACY.W.
Write narratives to develop real or imagined experiences or events using effective technique, relevant descriptive details, and well-structured event sequences.

- CCSS.ELA-LITERACY.W.
Use narrative techniques, such as dialogue, pacing, description, and reflection, to develop experiences, events, and/or characters.

ESSENTIAL QUESTIONS

- How do I use correct punctuation to indicate a break in my storyline, or saga?
- How can I use figurative language to bring my character to life?
- What is the difference between anthropomorphism and personification?
- Who is my audience? Who is going to be reading my story?
- What is the purpose of my story?
- How do I convey the purpose of my story through word choice and sequencing?
- What techniques can I use to introduce my characters?
- How do I tell a story with only dialogue?
- How can I use humor in the form of irony or puns to engage my audience?

APP INTEGRATIONS AND EXTENSIONS

Canva   edpuzzle   BOOK CREATOR

INTRODUCING #FOODSAGAS TO STUDENTS

#FoodSagas in English Classroom:
This year we are compiling a book of #foodsagas as a class. To create a food saga you simply snap a photo of your food or find food in Canva, personify the food by drawing human-like features on the image, give your food hero or villain a name, and create a story! You can even take it a step further and use an app like Chatterpix to make your food talk, ComicBook! app to create a comic, or turn your images into an animated gif! This is a fun way of addressing language conventions such as punctuation, active and passive voice, figurative language, and narrative compositions. Through a sequence of photos and narrative storytelling techniques your #foodsaga will demonstrate your mastery of language and writing standards outlined in the rubric.

DEMONSTRATING 8TH GRADE WRITING COMPETENCIES ONE MEAL AT A TIME!

CRITERIA

1. Each student should create and submit a visual narrative of at least 15-20 photos over the course the unit, lasting 3 weeks.
2. The photos should include figurative language, including but not limited to personification of food and onomatopoeia.
3. The narrative must be crafted in a well-structured sequence and communicated through dialogue that drives the plot forward.
4. The author's purpose should be clear.
5. The text must demonstrate proper punctuation and writing conventions as outlined in the rubric.
6. The narrative must contain examples of active and passive voice.
7. Students will use Book Creator to create a book on the FoodSaga book shelf. Join code: SB8DL8R (you will create your own book shelf for your class)
8. Each student must provide 2 peer reviews and a self assessment using the #FoodSaga rubric google form.

Level Up: Get uber creative with your #foodsaga narrative by using an app like Chatterpix, or Facetalk to make your dialogue spoken (must still include written text with proper punctuation). Use Giphy, Canva, or Momento to turn your photos into animated Gifs.

TEMPLATE

SCAN TO PREVIEW THE WHOLE UNIT MADE IN BOOK CREATOR

SCAN ME

OBJECTIVES AND ASSIGNMENT CHECKLIST

OBJECTIVES
Generated by Font-Generator.com

Students will learn how to use irony in the context of a story.

Students will craft narratives around food.

Students will athropormorphize food, and give it a personality.

Students will learn how to properly use an ellipse and punctuate dialgue.

RESEARCH

Suggested conventions and search terms : narrative, irony, humor, personificati... passive voice, alliteration, purpose, audience, characterization.

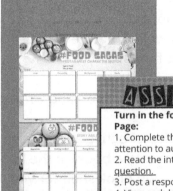

ASSIGNMENT CHECKLIST

Turn in the following through Classcraft Assignments in your Quest Page:
1. Complete the <u>Edpuzzle Video</u> on the short film "Bao," paying close attention to author's purpose and voice.
2. Read the interview from the Director of "Bao" and <u>answer the discussion question.</u>
3. Post a response on the <u>FoodSaga Padlet</u> on voice and audience.
4. View each lesson on the following language and writing conventions. Complete each activity<u>.</u>
  <u>-active vs passive voice</u>
  <u>-figurative language</u>
  <u>-punctuation</u>
  <u>-include puns or irony, in context.</u>
5. Review your <u>Rubric.</u>
5. Begin your <u>planning guide and storyboard</u>.
6. <u>Submit a visual narrative of at least 6-8 photos</u> that meet the requirements of the rubric.
7. <u>Submit 5 peer reviews and a self assessment</u> using the #FoodSaga rubric google form.

RUBRIC

Your Narrative will be graded on the following rubric.

	4	3	2	1
Punctuation: -commas -quotation marks in dialogue. **(20 points)**	Uses punctuation to enhance the quality of the story.	Uses punctuation correctly 95% of the time.	Uses punctuation correctly 75 % of the time	Uses punctuation correctly less than 50% of the time.
Conventions: --Proper nouns capitalized. -Sentence structure matches purpose. **(20 points)**	Uses conventions to enhance the quality of the story.	Uses conventions correctly 95% of the time.	Uses conventions correctly 75% of the time.	Uses conventions correctly 50% of the time.
Style: -Images -Figurative Language -Diction -Syntax **(20 points)**	Uses stylistic elements consistently to enhance the quality of the story.	Uses stylistic elements occasionally to enhance the story.	Uses stylistic elements a few times to enhance the story.	Seldom uses stylistic elements to enhance the story.
Narrative Development: -plot: sequence of events (beginning, middle, end) -historical accuracy **(20 points)**	Sequence of events is not only clear, but uses a well organized plot line to enhance the story.	Sequence of events is clear. Plot has a beginning, middle, and end.	Sequence of events is mostly clear, but may become a little confusing once or twice.	Sequence of events is hard to follow or there is little to no plot.
Images/Creativity/ Effort: **(20 points)**	Story is very clever, creative, cute, and catchy. Very original.	Story is creative and engaging.	Story has moments of creativity.	Story lacks effort or creativity.

SAMPLE OF STUDENT WORK

CHECK OUT THE BOOKSHELF AND BROWSE STORIES BY STUDENTS JOINING USING THIS CODE: SB8DL8R

QR CODE TO STUDENT BOOK

PODCAST UNIT

DESCRIPTION

With digital media becoming a more prominent form of communicating with the world, media production is a necessary skill in today's society and podcasting naturally lends itself to interdisciplinary connections. Podcasting focuses on the act of disseminating information through storytelling in an audio format. As students write narratives with logical sequences, plan, record, and mix audio, they will learn the technical side of producing and publishing a podcast, while being cognizant of the new format and audience they are producing for. It can be adapted to any content area! The purpose of this project is to write a narrative confessional in the style of Edgar Allan Poe, paying close attention to developing theme, mood, and creating a logical sequence of events through the lens of an unreliable narrator. Students will then leverage the power of podcasting and develop a basic understanding of podcast production.

LEARNING GOALS

- Students will write confessional narratives in the style of Edgar Allan Poe focusing on theme, mood, and the sequence of events as told through the perspective of first person unreliable narrator.
- Students will become familiar with a podcast format and the anchor.fm editing and publishing platform.
- Students will record and edit their podcasts, include music, sound effects, and design a cover. They will then publish their podcast on anchor.fm.

DOK LEVEL (4)

TYPE OF ASSIGNMENT
Individual/Group

GRADE LEVEL
3-8

DURATION
3 Weeks

STANDARDS

CCSS.ELA-LITERACY.W.
Write narratives to develop real or imagined experiences or events using effective technique, relevant descriptive details, and well-structured event sequences.
CCSS.ELA-LITERACY.SL.
Adapt speech to a variety of contexts and tasks, demonstrating command of formal English when indicated or appropriate.

ESSENTIAL QUESTIONS

- What are the elements of gothic literature?
- How can I write a narrative that develops real or imagined experiences or events using effective technique, well-chosen details, and well-structured event sequences?
- How does a speaker use point of view, reasoning, and use of evidence and rhetoric, assessing the stance, premises, links among ideas, word choice, points of emphasis, and tone used in a narrative piece?
- How can I use technology, including the Internet, to produce, publish, and update individual or shared writing products, taking advantage of technology's capacity to link to other information and to display information flexibly and dynamically?
- Why is it important to include variety of techniques to sequence events in a text so that they build on one another to create a coherent whole?

APP INTEGRATIONS AND EXTENSIONS

   Anchor

 Canva edpuzzle BOOK CREATOR

STUDENT ASSIGNMENT HANDOUT

"There is a radical error, I think, in the usual mode of constructing a story ... I first established in mind the climax."~ Edgar Allan Poe

'How many good books suffer neglect through the inefficiency of their beginnings!' ~Edgar Allan Poe

The Narrative Assignment

You will write your own confessional narrative story or poem that is inspired by the writing of Edgar Allan Poe. Your narrative must include an unreliable narrator, just like the narrators in Poe's works, with an underlying theme of madness. Your narrative should include objects or images that act as symbols or represent other ideas. Finally, you must use complex sentence structures, emphasized punctuation, and descriptive words to invoke gothic literature elements and imagery. Poe's "The Tell-Tale Heart," was 2100 words, so the length of your story should be at least1500 words.

How to write like POE:

- ❏ **Antihero:** First person narrative, madness, insanity and unreliable. There is often a contradiction between what the character says/does.
- ❏ **Characterization:** Often the protagonist is the bad guy and the antagonist is the good guy!
- ❏ **A Crime/confession:** single incident, such as the burial of a not-yet-dead person, the murder of an innocent, or a prisoner's attempt to escape through the lens of a narrator trying to explain or justify their actions.
- ❏ **Dualistic theme:** While the main theme is Madness, there is often an underlying theme of imprisonment, or loss of control.
- ❏ **Setting:** Ambiguity of time and place. It provides a universality and timelessness to Poe's stories, which have helped maintain their popularity to this day.
- ❏ **Horror:** The true horror is the madness and darkness of the human mind, but there are subsidiary fears Poe injects: fear of being buried alive, disease, an evil eye, a cat, etc,
- ❏ **Language and STYLE:** Flowery compound sentences. Adverbs, superfluous use of exclamation points & em dashes-and the thesaurus is your friend!

QR CODE TO ASSIGNMENT

TEMPLATE

SCAN TO PREVIEW THE WHOLE UNIT MADE IN BOOK CREATOR

SCAN ME

OBJECTIVES AND ASSIGNMENT CHECKLIST

Podcast Requirements

1. Working in pairs students should record a [ ] in length.
2. Each episode must follow the Poecast epis[ ]
3. Episode should be edited and free of error[ ]
4. Episode should include a title, podcast intr[ ] statement, at least one Poe inspired narrativ[ ] debrief on the project answering the five que[ ] format.
5. Have unique podcast cover art for the epis[ ]
6. Include royalty free music (plenty available[ ] contributes to the mood of the story.
7. Include the PoeCast Closing Paragraph ou[ ]
8. Be published using Anchor.fm.
9. Add link to podcast to your digital noteboo[ ]

Define: Explore Resources and Address Knowledge Gaps

Lesson One: Narrative Writing	Lesson Two: First Person Perspective	Lesson Three: The Style and Language of Poe
Lesson Four: Writing like Poe	Lesson Five: Theme to Craft a Story	Lesson Six: Using Symbols in Storytelling
Lesson Seven: What is a Podcast?	Lesson Eight: Using Sound to Create Mood	Lesson Six: Podcast Cover Art
	Lesson Nine: Anchor.fm Guide	

Task: Explore the resources above on narrative writing, theme, symbolism, Poe's language and style, sound design, and podcasting to address any knowledge gaps that you might have. The resources are a compilation of instructional videos, articles, and lessons to help address the skills needed to complete this project.

SAMPLE OF PODCAST COVERS AND STUDENT WORK

SCAN TO
LISTEN TO
THE MURDER
HOTEL
BY ELEANOR

WANTED SHAPES!

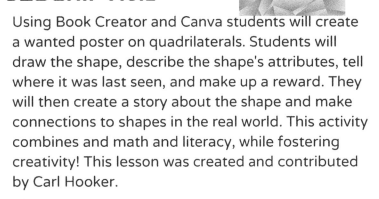

Quadrilaterals on the Loose!

Contributed by Carl Hooker

DOK LEVEL (3)

TYPE OF ASSIGNMENT

Individual

GRADE LEVEL

3-5

DURATION

1-2 hours

STANDARDS

CCSS.MATH.CONTENT.3.G.A.1 Understand that shapes in different categories (e.g., rhombuses, rectangles, and others) may share attributes (e.g., having four sides), and that the shared attributes can define a larger category (e.g., quadrilaterals). Recognize rhombuses, rectangles, and squares as examples of quadrilaterals, and draw examples of quadrilaterals that do not belong to any of these subcategories.

ESSENTIAL QUESTIONS

- What attributes do different shapes have?
- What is a quadrilateral?
- What examples of my shape can I find in the real world?

APP INTEGRATIONS AND EXTENSIONS

Canva

BOOK CREATOR

DESCRIPTION

Using Book Creator and Canva students will create a wanted poster on quadrilaterals. Students will draw the shape, describe the shape's attributes, tell where it was last seen, and make up a reward. They will then create a story about the shape and make connections to shapes in the real world. This activity combines and math and literacy, while fostering creativity! This lesson was created and contributed by Carl Hooker.

LEARNING GOALS

- Students will understand that shapes are categorized differently.
- Students will create a story about a quadrilateral and describe its attributes.
- Students will compare and contrast their shapes with their peers.
- Students will make connections to real world examples of shapes.

TEACHING TIPS

Create your own book shelf in Book Creator and create a template book for your activity. Invite students to join the book shelf and duplicate the template. You could also just make stories in Canva alone and not use book creator.

SCAN TO PREVIEW THE WHOLE ACTIVITY MADE IN BOOK CREATOR

SCAN ME

BOOK CREATOR TEMPLATE

Quadrilaterals on the Loose!

OBJECTIVES AND ASSIGNMENT CHECKLIST

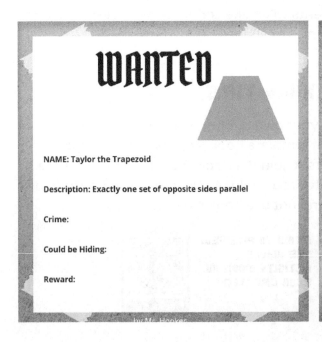

WANTED

NAME: Taylor the Trapezoid

Description: Exactly one set of opposite sides parallel

Crime:

Could be Hiding:

Reward:

by Mr. Hooker

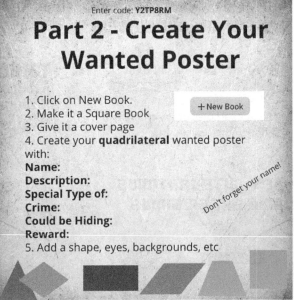

Enter code: **Y2TP8RM**

Part 2 - Create Your Wanted Poster

1. Click on New Book.
2. Make it a Square Book
3. Give it a cover page
4. Create your **quadrilateral** wanted poster with:
Name:
Description:
Special Type of:
Crime:
Could be Hiding:
Reward:
5. Add a shape, eyes, backgrounds, etc

+ New Book

Don't forget your name!

SAMPLE OF WANTED SHAPES AND STUDENT WORK

Name: Silly Square

Description: 2 pairs of parallel sides, 4 sides of equal length, and 4 right angles.
Special Type of: Rectangle

Crime: Breaking through pizza shop windows and eating pizza out of people's pizza boxes.

Could be hiding: In a window or a pizza box.

Reward: 100 pizzas and $1,000!

ADELE F.

Name: Ruby Rhombus
Description:She looks parallelogram and purple and four side and corners
Special Type of:Rhombus,parallelogram,square
Crime:putting two slice of pizza making a rhombus
Could be Hiding: Two slice of pizza
Reward:100,000,000,000

MANIFEST DESTINY

MANIFEST DESTINY:
westward expansion

DESCRIPTION

This unit covers a ton of key terms, important battles, and historical figures covering five decades of US history. The driving question for the entire unit is "Was Manifest Destiny Justified?" The intent was to "Manifest Destiny," the idea that Americans were destined by God to spread civilization and democracy westward across the continent. However, the impact had negative effects on Native Americans, African Americans, and immigrants from Mexico and China, though women saw improvements.

In this unit students will learn about Westward Expansion through the lens of game design. Similar to Oregon Trail, they will design a game that relies heavily on narrative story telling mechanics and focuses on communicating historical events through the perspectives of marginalized groups; African Americans, Native Americans, Women, and Immigrants. Each level will focus on a specific decade of Westward expansion.

LEARNING GOALS

- Students will demonstrate impacts of Westward Expansion on Native Americans, Black People, Immigrants, and Women through dialogue.
- Students will design various game levels that visually compare and contrast the intent of Westward Expansion with the impacts it had on marginalized groups.
- Students will craft an argumentative claim as to whether the intent behind Westward Expansion justified the ultimate impacts on particular identity groups.

DOK LEVEL 4

TYPE OF ASSIGNMENT

Individual/Group

GRADE LEVEL

8-11

DURATION

4 weeks

STANDARDS

- 8.G.GR.1 Use maps and other geographic representations, geospatial technologies, and spatial thinking to analyze settlement patterns in the United States from the Colonial Era to Reconstruction from 1600-1877.
- 8.H.CH.1 Explain the role changing political, social and economic perspectives had on the lives of diverse groups of people in the Colonial Era.
- 8.H.CH.2 Analyze how social and ideological philosophies impacted various movements in the United States from the Colonial Era to Reconstruction from 1600-1877

ESSENTIAL QUESTIONS

- How did Westward Expansion impact marginalized groups?
- What was Manifest Destiny?
- What was the intent of Manifest Destiny?
- Was westward expansion justified?
- How can I take my knowledge of westward expansion and turn it into a video game?

APP INTEGRATIONS AND EXTENSIONS

TEACHING TIPS

This unit can span four weeks if students build out all four levels. I recommend grouping students into groups of four and have them work together to build the same game. First, have students explore key terms, define them, and research the impact that westward expansion on each of the four marginalized groups. Each level will focus on a different marginalized identity. Each group should have access to all the planning guides, and each group member is responsible for one of the levels. After they define the key terms, they should begin writing the narrative for their level, storyboard it, and then move to background and character design. The narrative will be communicated through character dialogue, and they will need to know enough about the history of this time to determine who the enemies are, the coins, and how they can use storyblocks to move along the plot of the game. Make sure students complete the planning guide before they ever get access to Bloxels to ensure the learning and understanding of content is properly communicated, so their game will be accurate. Whether or not they actually finish the game isn't relevant, because if they complete the planning guide they should know the content well. Students will make a book in book creator showing their plans and then link their games. They can include video play narrations explaining the game mechanics and the thinking behind it.

SCAN QR CODE TO PREVIEW THE WHOLE ACTIVITY MADE IN CANVA

SAMPLE LEVEL DESIGN PAGES

LEVEL 1:
1820S MAT'S GENERAL STORE

Independence town square

WHAT IMPACT DID WESTWARD EXPANSION HAVE ON AFRICAN AMERICANS?

Back then Oregon Trail, Level 1 begins in Independence, Missouri in the 1820s at Mat's General Store. Your protagonist will begin preparing to go west. You will need to research the geography and location to inform your background design and setting. Next you will develop your character, and the enemies and friends that they will interact with. You will build story pieces/people that your novice will interact with to introduce the topic of Westward Expansion through dialogue. What will your cards be? What must your character need for their journey's success that they could collect along the way? You want to be sure to include information about significant terms, events, and people from this decade to be sure you are addressing the rubric requirements of the project. Now let's begin planning for game!

In your group you may consider dividing and conquering the design work of each part of the game. These are suggested roles below:

_____ Narrative Storyteller   _____ Icon Designer
_____ Background/Setting Designer   _____ Level Designer
_____ Enemy Designer   _____ Protagonist Designer

YOU HAVE DIED OF DYSENTERY

terms
- [ ] The Land Act of 1820
- [ ] Missouri Compromise of 1820
- [ ] Monroe Doctrine 1823
- [ ] James Monroe
- [ ] The Santa Fe Trail
- [ ] The Mormon Trail
- [ ] The Oregon Trail

LEVEL 1:
KEY TERMS AND FIGURES

terms
- [ ] The Land Act of 1820
- [ ] Missouri Compromise of 1820
- [ ] Monroe Doctrine 1823
- [ ] The Mormon Trail
- [ ] The Oregon Trail
- [ ] The Santa Fe Trail
- [ ] James Monroe

The Land Act of 1820

Missouri Compromise of 1820

Monroe Doctrine 1823

The Mormon Trail

The Oregon Trail

The Santa Fe Trail

James Monroe

LEVEL 1-A:
GAME DESIGN OUTLINE

[VIDEO game]

Directions: Use this sheet to brainstorm and plan an overview or outline of your game!

What is the setting of your game like? Brush up geography and where your level is taking place on the map. Include the time.

Who will the hero or protagonist of your game be?

Who will the enemies be? Think of these potential enemies your hero could come into contact with on their journey. Make historically accurate.

What is potential currency in your game? Your game has to have coins, but you can create what those are. Think back. What does your hero need to successfully complete the journey? List three.

Story blocks. What characters or item will your hero encounter on the way to help tell the historical narrative? Is certain people? Historical figures? Inanimate objects?

Power-ups. What could your character use to restore health, or get special powers. How will you visually represent this?

Power-ups. What could your character use to restore health, or get special powers. How will you visually represent this?

LEVEL 1: PLANNING GUIDE:
STORYBOARD

DIRECTIONS
Visualize your story by sketching out some scenes that will take place in your game. Who will protagonist meet? How will you communicate the key terms and events from this decade visually and chronologically?

GAME STORYBOARD
Using the boxes below, draw and describe the scenes in your game.

LEVEL 1: PLANNING GUIDE:
NARRATIVE STORYTELLING

DIRECTIONS
You will use the definitions from your key terms to write a ... happen in each level. A narrative ... takes place usually in chronological ... or bring together all of terms ... game that is historically accurate

... Who introduces the exposition? What is ... during this time? What is happening?

terms
- [ ] The Land Act of 1820
- [ ] Missouri Compromise of 1820
- [ ] Monroe Doctrine 1823
- [ ] James Monroe
- [ ] The Santa Fe Trail
- [ ] The Mormon Trail
- [ ] The Oregon Trail

SAMPLE OF STUDENT WORK

As part of the assessment you can download PDF's of the storyblock dialogue to ensure they used key terms and content in their game. Students can play each others games at the end of the unit. You can even create a classroom arcade where other teachers or parents can come in and play student games.

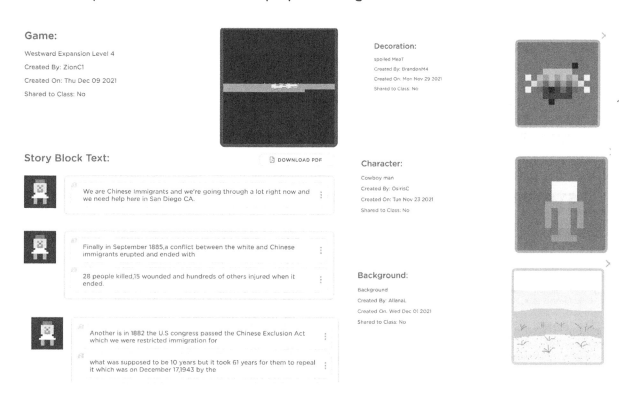

Game:

Westward Expansion Level 4
Created By: ZionC1
Created On: Thu Dec 09 2021
Shared to Class: No

Decoration:

spoiled MeaT
Created By: BrandonM4
Created On: Mon Nov 29 2021
Shared to Class: No

Story Block Text: 📄 DOWNLOAD PDF

We are Chinese Immigrants and we're going through a lot right now and we need help here in San Diego CA.

Finally in September 1885, a conflict between the white and Chinese immigrants erupted and ended with

28 people killed, 15 wounded and hundreds of others injured when it ended.

Character:

Cowboy man
Created By: OsirisC
Created On: Tue Nov 23 2021
Shared to Class: No

Another is in 1882 the U.S congress passed the Chinese Exclusion Act which we were restricted immigration for

what was supposed to be 10 years but it took 61 years for them to repeal it which was on December 17,1943 by the

Background:

Background
Created By: AllanaL
Created On: Wed Dec 01 2021
Shared to Class: No

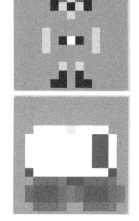

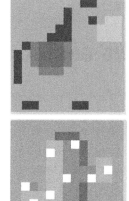

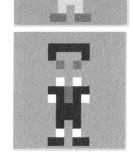

SCAN FOR BOOK CREATOR TEMPLATE

📱 SCAN ME

LITERATURE CIRCLES

DESCRIPTION

Literature circles with Canva and Book Creator are a great way to increase student discussion and engagement with a novel or text through multiple lenses or roles. The roles in this particular template are: word wizard, passage master, summarizer, connector, and discussion director. Roles aren't necessarily needed for a literature circle to be successful, but are included in this lesson.

This strategy allows students to apply skills such as reading comprehension, vocabulary, text analysis, and more depending on how the teacher customizes the tasks to target the skills they are seeking to observe and develop. It also gives students the power of voice to communicate their connections to a text, fosters a culture of inclusion, and multiple perspectives can lead to new understandings.

Literature circles are comprised of small peer-led discussion groups that are reading the same book and have all students participate through the demands of each role.

LEARNING GOALS

- Students will identity the qualities of a good discussion.
- Students will model strategies that encourage conversation about difficult topics.
- Students will practice active listening.
- Students will come to consensus regarding a shared list of discussion norms.
- Students will engage in meta-conversation about discussion techniques.

DOK LEVEL (4)

TYPE OF ASSIGNMENT

Group/Collaborative/Analysis

GRADE LEVEL

K-12

DURATION

Duration of Text/Novel
(depending on length of text)

STANDARDS

CCSS.ELA-LITERACY.SL.
Engage effectively in a range of collaborative discussions (one-on-one, in groups, and teacher-led) with diverse partners on grade 6 topics, texts, and issues, building on others' ideas and expressing their own clearly.
CCSS.ELA-LITERACY.SL.
Interpret information presented in diverse media and formats (e.g., visually, quantitatively, orally) and explain how it contributes to a topic, text, or issue under study.
CCSS.ELA-LITERACY.SL.
Present claims and findings, sequencing ideas logically and using pertinent descriptions, facts, and details to accentuate main ideas or themes; use appropriate eye contact, adequate volume, and clear pronunciation.
CCSS.ELA-LITERACY.SL.
Include multimedia components (e.g., graphics, images, music, sound) and visual displays in presentations to clarify information.

ESSENTIAL QUESTIONS

- What does a good discussion sound/look like?
- What is the individual's role in making a discussion run smoothly?
- What strategies can be used to deepen our conversations about books?

APP INTEGRATIONS AND EXTENSIONS

TEACHING TIPS

When using literature circles to teach texts, novels, and short stories, you will want to first introduce students to each role using the Literature Circles Roles and Responsibilities presentation available by QR code at the bottom of the page. Next, you will want to determine how to divide the book. For longer texts, like The Outsiders, or Night, you may wish to divide it by page numbers or chapters. For The Outsiders I broke the text into four sections and had students cover three chapters in each section. When students went to a new section of the project I had them switch roles. The idea is to have students rotate through each role in order to engage with the text in different ways, while hitting on various standards. For shorter texts, or younger students, you may want each student to create a book creator book on the text instead of working in groups and complete all the roles individually. You may also want to offer graphic organizers to scaffold each role. I like to create a master template for students to duplicate and customize with the sections of the book predetermined by me. At the end of each section, I recommend students coming to discuss the text and recording the conversation via Flipgrid or another tool to encourage on topic discussion and collaboration between group members.

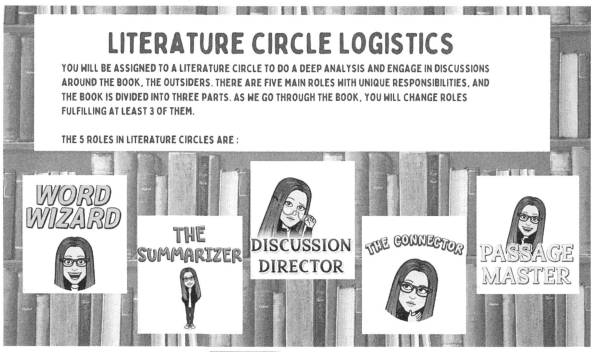

LITERATURE CIRCLE LOGISTICS

YOU WILL BE ASSIGNED TO A LITERATURE CIRCLE TO DO A DEEP ANALYSIS AND ENGAGE IN DISCUSSIONS AROUND THE BOOK, THE OUTSIDERS. THERE ARE FIVE MAIN ROLES WITH UNIQUE RESPONSIBILITIES, AND THE BOOK IS DIVIDED INTO THREE PARTS. AS WE GO THROUGH THE BOOK, YOU WILL CHANGE ROLES FULFILLING AT LEAST 3 OF THEM.

THE 5 ROLES IN LITERATURE CIRCLES ARE :

WORD WIZARD

THE SUMMARIZER

DISCUSSION DIRECTOR

THE CONNECTOR

PASSAGE MASTER

SCAN TO FOR THE LITERATURE CIRCLE ROLES AND RESPONSIBILITIES TEMPLATE

SAMPLE ROLES FROM LITERATURE CIRCLE

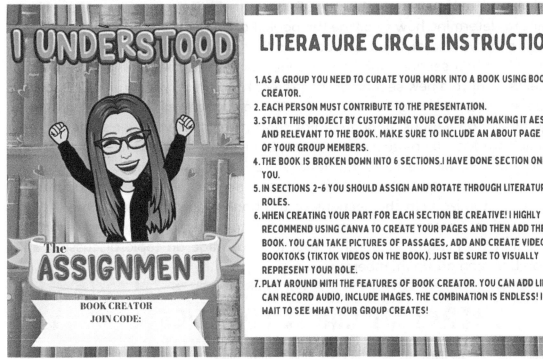

LITERATURE CIRCLE INSTRUCTIONS

1. AS A GROUP YOU NEED TO CURATE YOUR WORK INTO A BOOK USING BOOK CREATOR.
2. EACH PERSON MUST CONTRIBUTE TO THE PRESENTATION.
3. START THIS PROJECT BY CUSTOMIZING YOUR COVER AND MAKING IT AESTHETIC AND RELEVANT TO THE BOOK. MAKE SURE TO INCLUDE AN ABOUT PAGE WITH ALL OF YOUR GROUP MEMBERS.
4. THE BOOK IS BROKEN DOWN INTO 6 SECTIONS. I HAVE DONE SECTION ONE FOR YOU.
5. IN SECTIONS 2-6 YOU SHOULD ASSIGN AND ROTATE THROUGH LITERATURE CIRCLE ROLES.
6. WHEN CREATING YOUR PART FOR EACH SECTION BE CREATIVE! I HIGHLY RECOMMEND USING CANVA TO CREATE YOUR PAGES AND THEN ADD THEM TO THE BOOK. YOU CAN TAKE PICTURES OF PASSAGES, ADD AND CREATE VIDEOS, BOOKTOKS (TIKTOK VIDEOS ON THE BOOK). JUST BE SURE TO VISUALLY REPRESENT YOUR ROLE.
7. PLAY AROUND WITH THE FEATURES OF BOOK CREATOR. YOU CAN ADD LINKS, YOU CAN RECORD AUDIO, INCLUDE IMAGES. THE COMBINATION IS ENDLESS! I CAN'T WAIT TO SEE WHAT YOUR GROUP CREATES!

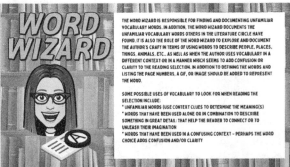

THE WORD WIZARD IS RESPONSIBLE FOR FINDING AND DOCUMENTING UNFAMILIAR VOCABULARY WORDS. IN ADDITION, THE WORD WIZARD DOCUMENTS THE UNFAMILIAR VOCABULARY WORDS OTHERS IN THE LITERATURE CIRCLE HAVE FOUND. IT IS ALSO THE ROLE OF THE WORD WIZARD TO EXPLORE AND DOCUMENT THE AUTHOR'S CRAFT IN TERMS OF USING WORDS TO DESCRIBE PEOPLE, PLACES, THINGS, ANIMALS, ETC., AS WELL AS WHEN THE AUTHOR USES VOCABULARY IN A DIFFERENT CONTEXT OR IN A MANNER WHICH SEEMS TO ADD CONFUSION OR CLARITY TO THE READING SELECTION. IN ADDITION TO DEFINING THE WORDS AND LISTING THE PAGE NUMBERS, A GIF, OR IMAGE SHOULD BE ADDED TO REPRESENT THE WORD.

SOME POSSIBLE USES OF VOCABULARY TO LOOK FOR WHEN READING THE SELECTION INCLUDE:
* UNFAMILIAR WORDS (USE CONTEXT CLUES TO DETERMINE THE MEANING(S)
* WORDS THAT HAVE BEEN USED ALONE OR IN COMBINATION TO DESCRIBE SOMETHING IN GREAT DETAIL: THAT HELP THE READER TO CONNECT OR TO UNLEASH THEIR IMAGINATION
* WORDS THAT HAVE BEEN USED IN A CONFUSING CONTEXT – PERHAPS THE WORD CHOICE ADDS CONFUSION AND/OR CLARITY

THE PASSAGE MASTER IS RESPONSIBLE FOR FINDING AND DOCUMENTING KEY PASSAGES FOUND THROUGHOUT THE READING SELECTION. IN ADDITION, THE PASSAGE MASTER DOCUMENTS THE PASSAGES OTHER GROUP MEMBERS FIND MEMORABLE. IN DOING SO, THE PASSAGE MASTER IS FOCUSING ON THE LITERARY MERITS OF THE SELECTION, SUCH AS IMAGERY, SENSORY LANGUAGE, AND FIGURATIVE LANGUAGE.

SOME KEY CHARACTERISTICS TO LOOK FOR WHEN CHOOSING PASSAGES INCLUDE:

* PASSAGES THAT PROVIDE INSIGHT INTO THE JUDGMENTS, FEELINGS, EMOTIONS OR ACTIONS OF A CHARACTER (SUCH AS THOUGHTS OR DIALOGUE).
* PASSAGES THAT PROVIDE AN "AHA" EXPERIENCE FOR THE READER.
* PASSAGES IN WHICH KEY STORY ELEMENTS ARE REVEALED.
* PASSAGES THAT DEMONSTRATE PERSONAL REVELATION OR WISDOM ON BEHALF OF A CHARACTER.
* PASSAGES THAT ARE PARTICULARLY GOOD AT DESCRIBING PEOPLE, PLACES, THINGS, ANIMALS, EMOTIONS, FEELINGS-ANY SENSORY LANGUAGE OR IMAGERY.

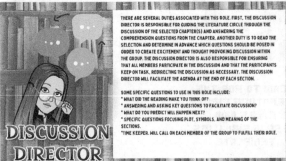

THERE ARE SEVERAL DUTIES ASSOCIATED WITH THIS ROLE. FIRST, THE DISCUSSION DIRECTOR IS RESPONSIBLE FOR GUIDING THE LITERATURE CIRCLE THROUGH THE DISCUSSION OF THE SELECTED CHAPTER(S) AND ANSWERING THE COMPREHENSION QUESTIONS FROM THE CHAPTER. ANOTHER DUTY IS TO READ THE SELECTION AND DETERMINE IN ADVANCE WHICH QUESTIONS SHOULD BE POSED IN ORDER TO CREATE EXCITEMENT AND THOUGHT PROVOKING DISCUSSION WITHIN THE GROUP. THE DISCUSSION DIRECTOR IS ALSO RESPONSIBLE FOR ENSURING THAT ALL MEMBERS PARTICIPATE IN THE DISCUSSION AND THAT THE PARTICIPANTS KEEP ON TASK, REDIRECTING THE DISCUSSION AS NECESSARY. THE DISCUSSION DIRECTOR WILL FACILITATE THE AGENDA AT THE END OF EACH SECTION.

SOME SPECIFIC QUESTIONS TO USE IN THIS ROLE INCLUDE:
* WHAT DID THE READING MAKE YOU THINK OF?
* ANSWERING AND ASKING KEY QUESTIONS TO FACILITATE DISCUSSION?
* WHAT DO YOU PREDICT WILL HAPPEN NEXT?
* SPECIFIC QUESTIONS FOCUSING PLOT, SYMBOLS, AND MEANING OF THE SECTIONS.
* TIME KEEPER. WILL CALL ON EACH MEMBER OF THE GROUP TO FULFILL THEIR ROLE.

TO PROVIDE A SUBJECTIVE AND QUICK READING SUMMARY IS AN IMPORTANT SKILL. IT IS THE JOB OF THE SUMMARIZER TO CREATE SUCH A SUMMARY AND READ IT TO THEIR GROUP. A SUMMARY SHOULD BE MORE THAN JUST A COUPLE LINES. SUMMARIES MUST CONTAIN IMPORTANT PLOT ELEMENTS AND CHARACTER NOTES. THEY SHOULD HIGHLIGHT THE MOST ESSENTIAL MOMENTS OF THE CHAPTER(S); WITHOUT THESE MOMENTS, THE CHAPTERS WOULD NOT MAKE SENSE. THE SUMMARIZER ALSO FUNCTIONS AS THE TASK MASTER, AND SHOULD TAKE NOTES AND SUMMARIZE THE INTERACTIONS OF EACH GROUP MEMBER.

RESPONSIBILITIES FOR THE SUMMARIZER WHEN READING THE SELECTION INCLUDE:
* KEY CONCLUSIONS THE GROUP HAS COME TO AS A RESULT OF THE DISCUSSION.
* KEY POINTS IN THE READING SELECTION THAT HAVE THE GROUP EXCITED, CURIOUS, OR THAT THEY JUST FIND INTERESTING.
* PASSAGES WHERE HUMOR HAS BEEN USED.
* KEY PASSAGES DISCUSSED. (FROM THE DISCUSSION LEAD BY THE PASSAGE KEEPER)
* VOCABULARY WORDS. (FROM THE DISCUSSION LEAD BY THE WORD WIZARD)
* PREDICTIONS THE GROUP IS MAKING AFTER READING THE SELECTION.
* HOW THE GROUP HAS CONNECTED THE READING SELECTION. (FROM THE DISCUSSION LEAD BY THE CONNECTOR)

SAMPLE OF STUDENT WORK

These are samples from an 8th grade led literature circle on the book Night, by Elie Wiesel. Literature circles hit the speaking and listening standards as students engage in rich discussions. Included below, also are some of the conversations from 7th grade students on The Outsiders via Flipgrid.

SCAN FOR ACCESS TO BOOK CREATOR BOOKSHELF

48 views · 0 comments · 7.7 hours of engagement

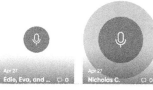

Outsiders Literature Circles Ch 5-8

17 responses · 48 views · 2 comments · 7.7 hours of discussion

Film a 10 min discussion of chapters 5-8 of "The Outsiders" using your literature circle role.

Summarizer (2 min)
–summarize key events
–summarize interactions of group members

Word Wizard (1 min)
–slang
–words that resonated
–vocab
–motifs

Discussion Director (3 min)
–discussion of big topics
–Key events
–themes
–Predictions

Connector (2 mins)
–text to self
–text to society
–text to world
–past to present

Passage Master (2 mins)
–shocking passages
–important to conflict
–plot
–theme.
With any time left over wrap up.

FLIPGRID VIDEO OF LITERATURE CIRCLE GROUP DISCUSSION

GRAPHIC ORGANIZERS

TO ACCESS ALL THE TEMPLATES IN THIS SECTION
SCAN THE QR CODE OR GO TO THE WEBSITE BELOW.

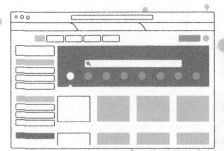

SCAN ME

WWW.TEACHERGOALS.COM/CANVATEMPLATES

GRAPHIC ORGANIZERS

DESCRIPTION

Graphic organizers help students visually demonstrate the relationships between facts, ideas, and key concepts. They enable students to comprehend and internalize new learning in an organized fashion. In this section of student templates I am going to provide search keywords for each type of organizer and an example of how to use it in the classroom. The standards included in the column to the left focus on common core Reading Information Texts, but can be adapted to content specific learning targets.

LEARNING GOALS

- Students will visualize information in multimodal ways.
- Students will organize ideas and concepts.
- Students will infer the relationships between key contepts and terms.

TEACHING TIPS

The essential questions will also change based on the content and grade level as well as the DOK level. Graphic organizers can range from a DOK1 to DOK4 depending on the task and experience you are creating for students.

QR CODE TO TEMPLATES ARE AVAILABLE ON EACH PAGE

DOK LEVEL

TYPE OF ASSIGNMENT
Individual/Group

GRADE LEVEL
K-12

STANDARDS

KWL Chart:
Common Core Standard: RI 3.1 – Ask and answer questions to demonstrate understanding of a text, referring explicitly to the text as the basis for the answers.

Venn Diagram:
RI 5.6 Analyze multiple accounts of the same event or topic, noting important similarities and differences in the point of view they represent.

Cornell Notes:
RI 6.8 Trace and evaluate the argument and specific claims in a text, distinguishing claims that are supported by reasons and evidence from claims that are not.

APP INTEGRATIONS AND EXTENSIONS

Canva

KWL TEMPLATES

When you search Canva templates for 'KWL' over 67 templates return. In the image below you can see the variety of templates that are available. The template at the bottom of the page includes a Genially embedded lesson on teaching the Butterfly Life Cycle and includes a KWL chart.

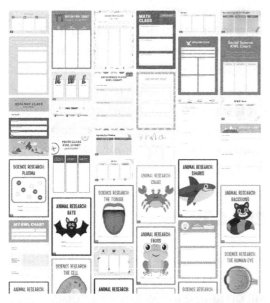

SCAN TO ACCESS ALL KWL TEMPLATES IN CANVA

QR CODE BUTTERFLY LIFE CYCLE TEMPLATE

CORNELL NOTES

When you search Canva templates for 'Cornell notes' only 4 templates return. One of the strategies I use with Cornell Notes is including the text in the left column with guiding questions in the right. Students then use the draw feature to annotate and highlight information relevant to the questions. I used this to teach relevant lyrics from the hit broadway musical Hamilton in my Revolutionary War unit.

4 templates

SCAN TO ACCESS ALL KWL TEMPLATES IN CANVA

QR CODE HAMILTON CORNELL NOTES TEMPLATE

SMART GOALS

When you search Canva templates for 'smart goals,' over 252 templates return. In the image below you can see the variety of templates that are available. The template at the bottom of the page is a template I created to help students set weekly goals and goals for project completion in my history class. There are also a ton of posters available to help teach students about setting a smart goal and what they are.

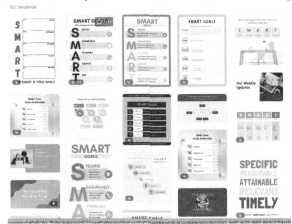

SMART GOALS

My goal is:

S	SPECIFIC	What do I want to happen?	
M	MEASUREABLE	How will I know when I have achieved my goal?	
A	ATTAINABLE	Is the goal realistic and how will I accomplish it?	
R	RELEVANT	Why is my goal important to me?	
T	TIMELY	What is my deadline for this goal?	

SCAN TO ACCESS ALL SMART GOALS TEMPLATES IN CANVA

QR CODE SMART GOALS TEMPLATE

VENN DIAGRAM

When you search Canva templates for 'Venn Diagram' over 79 templates return. In the image below you can see the variety of templates that are available. The template at the bottom of the page is on embedded in a lesson on teaching about activists, specifically Greta Thunberg and Malala Yousafzai. Jump forward to the Global Goals template section for the complete lesson!

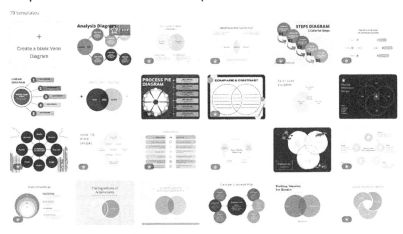

SCAN TO ACCESS ALL VENN DIAGRAM TEMPLATES IN CANVA

SCAN ME

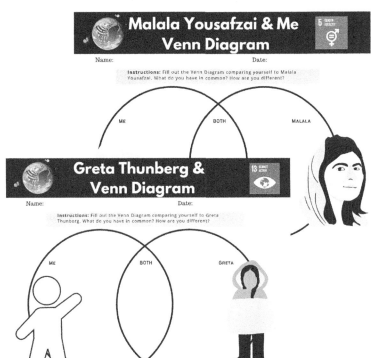

QR CODE VENN DIAGRAM ACTIVIST TEMPLATE

SCAN ME

DESIGN THINKING TEMPLATE

When you search Canva templates for 'design thinking,' over 1,571 templates return. Implementing the design thinking framework in your classroom is a great way to up the rigor to a DOK4 and have students identify problems and design solutions to those issues. Design thinking helps students develop empathy, insights and understandings, define problems as an actionable question, generate and visualize ideas, and develop prototypes/solutions, then test these design solutions. Check out the book, Zom-Be A Design thinker to introduce students younger students to the modes of design thinking! The student design thinking journal has a song to help littles learn design thinking.

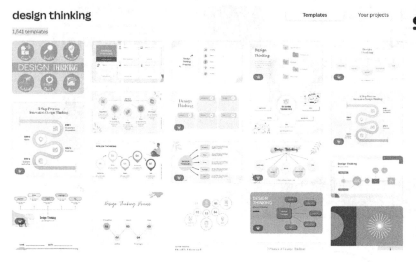

SCAN TO ACCESS ALL DESIGN THINKING TEMPLATES IN CANVA

SCAN ME

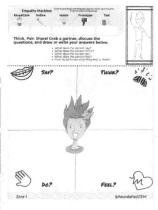

QR CODE TO DESIGN THINKING STUDENT JOURNAL TEMPLATE

SCAN ME

VIDEO AND ANIMATION TEMPLATES

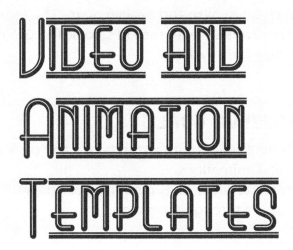

TO ACCESS ALL THE TEMPLATES IN THIS SECTION
SCAN THE QR CODE OR GO TO THE WEBSITE BELOW.

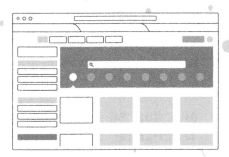

SCAN ME

WWW.TEACHERGOALS.COM/CANVATEMPLATES

STOP MOTION ANIMATION

DESCRIPTION

Within Canva you and your students can create stop motion animation movies for the purpose of digital storytelling across the curriculum. This engages students and gets them more involved throughout the learning process and puts them in the seat of creator. Students can create historical reenactments, create animations about habitats or life cycles, visualize and explain math. The example I have provided is with the kid's book The Great Eggscape by Jory John.

LEARNING GOALS

- Students will create a storyboard and plan their digital animations.
- Students will visually communicate their learning through animation.

TEACHING TIPS

When introducing animation to students start by showing them an exemplar. Explain that animation can be created by building a slide, duplicating it, and slightly moving the characters or elements on the page. To level up, students can add audio, voice recordings, and even use the draw feature to animate facial expressions and movement.

DOK LEVEL ②

TYPE OF ASSIGNMENT

Individual/Group/Video

GRADE LEVEL

K-12

ISTE STANDARDS

Common Core standards will vary depending on the content area and task you are asking students to perform

Empowered Learner
Students communicate clearly and express themselves creatively for a variety of purposes using the platforms, tools, styles, formats and digital media appropriate to their goals.

Creative Communicator
Students leverage technology to take an active role in choosing, achieving, and demonstrating competency in their learning goals, informed by the learning sciences.

ESSENTIAL QUESTIONS

- What visual elements do you notice in this story?
- What audio elements could you include for sound effects or to set the mood?
- How can you use multimedia to turn a text story into a digital animation?

APP INTEGRATIONS AND EXTENSIONS

QR CODE TO TEMPLATE

SCAN ME

Using the Seven Elements of Digital Storytelling will help you guide students to create rich digital creations. The seven elements are: Point of view, dramatic question, emotional content, pacing, soundtrack, economy, and voice. As they approach creating their animations, you can first have them complete a storyboard to scaffold their planning process. The storyboard can also have content specific questions to drive the project and ensure the project is aligned to content goals.

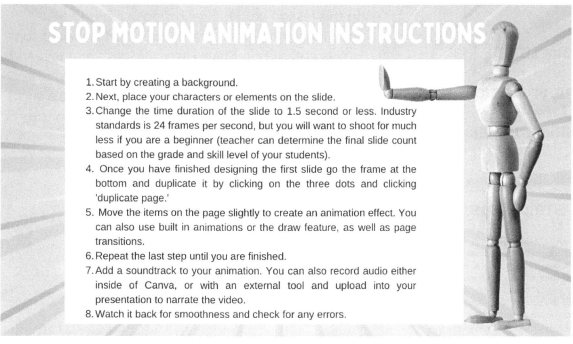

STOP MOTION ANIMATION INSTRUCTIONS

1. Start by creating a background.
2. Next, place your characters or elements on the slide.
3. Change the time duration of the slide to 1.5 second or less. Industry standards is 24 frames per second, but you will want to shoot for much less if you are a beginner (teacher can determine the final slide count based on the grade and skill level of your students).
4. Once you have finished designing the first slide go the frame at the bottom and duplicate it by clicking on the three dots and clicking 'duplicate page.'
5. Move the items on the page slightly to create an animation effect. You can also use built in animations or the draw feature, as well as page transitions.
6. Repeat the last step until you are finished.
7. Add a soundtrack to your animation. You can also record audio either inside of Canva, or with an external tool and upload into your presentation to narrate the video.
8. Watch it back for smoothness and check for any errors.

THE GREAT EGGSCAPE!

EXPOSITION- EVIDENCE & PAGE NUMBER	RISING ACTION: EVIDENCE & PAGE NUMBER
CLIMAX: EVIDENCE & PAGE NUMBER	FALLING ACTION: EVIDENCE & PAGE NUMBER
CONCLUSION: EVIDENCE & PAGE NUMBER	POINT OF VIEW:

QR CODE TO STORYBOARD

SCAN ME

BLACK HISTORY MONTH

DESCRIPTION

In this lesson students will choose a notable individual who is celebrated (or who they want to celebrate) during Black History Month and research their biographies. They will pick a quote from the person that resonates with them and create a short video explaining how they feel connected to the quote and what it means to them.

LEARNING GOALS

- Students will celebrate the contributions of art, poetry, music and inventions by African Americans through video creation.
- Students will explain their connections to quotes.

TEACHING TIPS

Black History Month isn't a one and done lesson. As educators we should ensure that the histories and texts that we teach are diverse and are integrated through our curriculum throughout the school year. When teaching this lesson consider sharing student videos throughout the year on the student news channel or on social media to give students an authentic audience.

DOK LEVEL 2

TYPE OF ASSIGNMENT
Individual/Group/Video

GRADE LEVEL
2-12

STANDARDS

CCSS.ELA-LITERACY.RI.
Ask and answer such questions as who, what, where, when, why, and how to demonstrate understanding of key details in a text.
CCSS.ELA-LITERACY.RI.
Describe the connection between a series of historical events, scientific ideas or concepts, or steps in technical procedures in a text.
CCSS.ELA-LITERACY.RI
Determine the meaning of words and phrases in a text relevant to a grade (x) topic or subject area.

ESSENTIAL QUESTIONS

- How can I use multimedia to celebrate the accomplishments of African Americans?
- How have Black People and Black History shaped the United States?

APP INTEGRATIONS AND EXTENSIONS

Canva

QR CODE TO TEMPLATE

ASSIGNMENT DETAILS

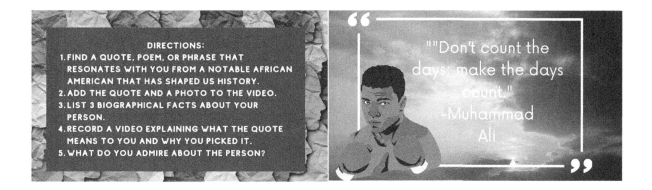

STUDENT WORK SAMPLES

The following student work samples are from 8th and 11th grade students in Louisville, Kentucky.

QR CODES TO STUDENT WORK SAMPLES

MATH LESSONS

TO ACCESS ALL THE TEMPLATES IN THIS SECTION
SCAN THE QR CODE OR GO TO THE WEBSITE BELOW.

SCAN ME

WWW.TEACHERGOALS.COM/CANVATEMPLATES

MARCH MATHNESS AND GRAPHING

DESCRIPTION

Canva has a ton of build in graphs and charts that makes visualizing data fun. If you search within elements, it is easy to find bar charts, line graphs, pie charts, scatter plots, and elements for pictograms to represent your data. They recently added the app 'Flourish' that can enhance your student graphs! Search for it in the 'more' section on the lefthand dashboard.

In this lesson, students will survey their classmates on which team they want to see win the National Championship. After they conduct a survey they will visualize the data in a pie chart and bar graph and compare and contrast the visual data that is being communicated in different ways.

LEARNING GOALS

- Students will conduct surveys and visualize data using graphs and pie charts.
- Students will compare and contrast graphs.

TEACHING TIPS

Start by introducing students to the various ways to visualize data. As an extension activity students can use the Quiver Vision app to play basketball virtually, and then write word problems (or create algebraic expressions) as another way to express numbers.

QR CODE TO TEMPLATE

SCAN ME

DOK LEVEL (2)

TYPE OF ASSIGNMENT
Individual/Group

GRADE LEVEL
K-3

STANDARDS

- CCSS.MATH.CONTENT.K.MD.A.2
Directly compare two objects with a measurable attribute in common, to see which object has "more of"/"less of" the attribute, and describe the difference. For example, directly compare the heights of two children and describe one child as taller/shorter.

- CCSS.MATH.CONTENT.1.MD.C.4
Organize, represent, and interpret data with up to three categories; ask and answer questions about the total number of data points, how many in each category, and how many more or less are in one category than in another.

- CCSS.MATH.CONTENT.2.MD.D.10
Draw a picture graph and a bar graph (with single-unit scale) to represent a data set with up to four categories. Solve simple put-together, take-apart, and compare problems1 using information presented in a bar graph.

ESSENTIAL QUESTIONS

- How can I use graphs and charts to visualize data?
- How do I represent data in visual ways?

APP INTEGRATIONS AND EXTENSIONS

ACTIVITIES

The content of this lesson can be changed from March Madness to measure just about anything you can think of. You could survey birthdays, cats vs dogs, favorite food, etc. Just change the theme by customizing the template and replacing the text with your survey choice. For K-1 you can eliminate two of the categories to make it age and standard appropriate.

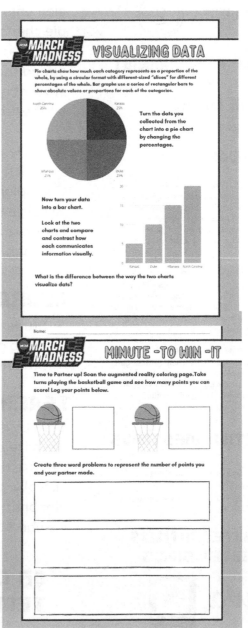

PIZZA FRACTIONS BROCHURE MENU

Contributed by Heather Brown

DESCRIPTION

In this lesson contributed by Heather Brown, students are to create a menu for a restaurant, but the catch is they have to create all of the serving sizes in fractions! Students select three different pizzas to divide into different numbers of slices, decide on a price per slice, and create deals to attract their customers by saving a little money! They also had to explain that the size of the whole makes the size of the pieces different even if it is the same fraction. Finally, they added other information that they learned about fractions.

This math lesson also includes persuasive writing, and helps foster design skills in students!

LEARNING GOALS

- Students will create a pizza menu applying their knowledge of fractions to slices.
- Students will draft a persuasive writing paragraph to convince consumers to dine at their establishment.

TEACHING TIPS

Start by walking students through the process of creating the "take-out menu" for their own pizza restaurant. You can have students work in small groups or individually. This activity should follow some formal instruction on fractions.

DOK LEVEL ③

TYPE OF ASSIGNMENT

Individual/Group/Application

GRADE LEVEL

3-5

STANDARDS

- CCSS.MATH.CONTENT.3.NF.A.1 Understand a fraction 1/b as the quantity formed by 1 part when a whole is partitioned into b equal parts; understand a fraction a/b as the quantity formed by a parts of size 1/b.
- CCSS.MATH.CONTENT.3.NF.A.3 Explain equivalence of fractions in special cases, and compare fractions by reasoning about their size.
- CCSS.MATH.CONTENT.3.NF.A.3.D Compare two fractions with the same numerator or the same denominator by reasoning about their size. Recognize that comparisons are valid only when the two fractions refer to the same whole. Record the results of comparisons with the symbols >, =, or <, and justify the conclusions, e.g., by using a visual fraction model.

ESSENTIAL QUESTIONS

- How do fractions of the same numerator and denominator compare relate to size?
- How does a part relate to the whole?
- What do I know about fractions?

APP INTEGRATIONS AND EXTENSIONS

Canva

QR CODE TO TEMPLATE

SCAN ME

ASSIGNMENT EXAMPLE

Deals!

Create deals for buying more than once slice of your pizzas using fractions! Include an equivalent fraction. Make sure the DEAL price is better than the original. View my examples for a better explanation.

Small Deal
Buy 2/4 or 1/2 of a small for $3!

Medium Deal
Buy 2/6 or 1/3 of a medium for $5!

Large Deal
Buy 4/10 or 2/5 of a large for $18!

COV
*PUT THE NAME
RESTAURANT
CHOOSE A PIZZA PHOT
ONTO THE PHOTOS TO

Choose a pizza picture and drag it onto this picture to replace it. Below use your persuasive skills to convince people to visit your pizzeria! DON'T FORGET TO DELETE INSTRUCTIONS AND WHAT YOU DON'T USE!

Freshest Pizza in Town
Persuade people here

Delete the pizza above and choose your own graphic from the elements tab.

Create a fake address, email, and website for your store. You may choose to have more than one. Use the samples below to guide you. Delete what you do not use

Chicago Location
123 Anywhere St., Any City, ST 12345
hello@reallygreatsite.com
www.reallygreatsite.com

New York Location
123 Anywhere St., Any City, ST 12345
hello@reallygreatsite.com
www.reallygreatsite.com

Menu

You need to include 3 different sizes of pizza and list how many slices are included in each size (choose even numbers). The price you list will be per slice of pizza. You may use mine as an example but you may NOT copy it.

Small
4 Slices
$2 per Slice

Medium
6 Slices
$3 per Slice

Large
10 Slices
$5 per Slice

Fraction Facts
Explain why 1/2 of a small pizza is not the same as 1/2 of a large pizza.
Explain what you enjoy about fractions.

STUDENT EXAMPLE

Monster Pizza

Don't let your stomach GROWL
Your stomach should not growl like a monster. Eat like a monster at Monster Pizza! Dig your teeth into pizza with eyes, teeth, and sometimes even spiders! It is the biggest secret around!

Where the Monsters Dine

Secret Location
Open your closet. Look under your pile of clothes. Say "take me to Monster Pizza". A monster will come get you and take you to the secret location.

Deals!

Friendly Deal
Buy 4/6 or 2/3 for $3!

Vampire Deal
Buy 4/8 or 1/2 for $10!

Fuzzy Deal
Buy 2/12 or 1/6 for $8!

Menu

Friendly
Slices
per Slice

Vampire
Slices
per Slice

Fuzzy
12 Slices
$5 per Slice

Fraction Facts
Think about a small pizza like a cupcake and a large pizza like a normal cake. I'd rather eat 1/2 of a normal cake than a cupcake because the whole is larger.

Monsters use fractions to compare! Like 3/10 monsters are scary but 7/10 are friendly. Or 3/5 monsters like math and 2/5 think it is scary.

QR CODE STUDENT EXAMPLE

SCAN ME

TELLING AND MEASURING TIME

DESCRIPTION

This activity plan will help students learn about clocks (analog & digital). They will learn how to tell & write the time in hours (e.g. 6:00pm), half-hours (e.g. 6:30pm) and minutes (e.g. 6:35pm). The activity plan includes links to informative videos about clocks as well as a "Time Telling Resource pack" to help explain key concepts to students. The Time Telling Resource Pack includes worksheets, time problems, guided notes, and time conversions materials. The teachers can also extend the activity plan further by asking students to record videos of themselves talking about their favorite time of day, or about a time they lost something that was important to them. The students can finish the lesson with the exciting Analog vs Digital scavenger hunt!

LEARNING GOALS

- Students will tell and write time using digital and analog clocks.
- Student will create and solve word problems involving time intervals.

TEACHING TIPS

This lesson template has a video that introduces analog vs digital. Begin by viewing the video as a class, and then have students use the handouts that are appropriate for the grade level. 3rd and 4th grade students can end with math mentals and timed conversions.

QR CODE TO TEMPLATE

DOK LEVEL ②

TYPE OF ASSIGNMENT
Group/Guided Practice

GRADE LEVEL
1-4

STANDARDS

- Grade 1: Tell & write time in hours and half-hours using analog & digital clocks.
- Grade 2: Tell & write time from analog and digital clocks to the nearest five minutes, using a.m. and p.m.
- Grade 3: Tell & write time to the nearest minute and measure time intervals in minutes. Solve word problems involving addition and subtraction of time intervals in minutes, e.g., by representing the problem on a number line diagram.
- Grade 4: Know relative sizes of measurement units within one system of units including km, m, cm; kg, g; lb, oz.; l, ml; hr, min, sec. Within a single system of measurement, express measurements in a larger unit in terms of a smaller unit.

ESSENTIAL QUESTIONS

- How are analog and digital clocks the same? How are they different?
- Why is it important to tell time?
- How can the hands on an analog clock be arranged to show time?
- What are different ways to say the times before and after the hour?

APP INTEGRATIONS AND EXTENSIONS

ACTIVITIES

Quiver Clock Page
QuiverVision

TELLING TIME

DIGITAL CLOCKS

How to Tell and Write Time (Digital and Analog Clocks)

02:00

two o'clock

Watch on YouTube

Directions
- Watch the video on telling time.
- Color the Quiver Vision Clock page.
- Scan it with the Quiver app and complete the guided notes page.
- Complete the 'What time is it?' and 'Word Problems' pages.
- Do the Time Conversions Math Mentals with students together.
- Find examples of real world applications that use analog and digital signals and add them to your scavenger hunt page.

Quiver Clock Guided Notes
QuiverVision

Name: _____ Date: _____

Guided Notes for AR Experience

Fill in the Blanks.

1. The _____ or _____ hand of a clock measures time in _____.

2. There are _____ seconds in a minute.

3 The _____ hand, or _____ hand measure bigger chunks of time called _____.

4. The _____ is the background of the clock where the number are located.

5. How many 10's are there in an hour?
[_____]

6. How many 5's are there in an hour?
[_____]

7. How did you come up with the answer to 5 and 6?
[_____]

© QuiverVision 2021

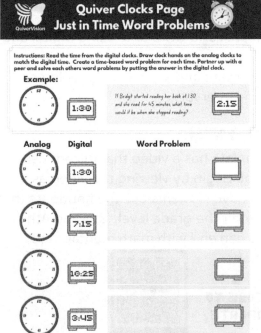

Quiver Clocks Page
Just in Time Word Problems
QuiverVision

Instructions: Read the time from the digital clocks. Draw clock hands on the analog clocks to match the digital time. Create a time-based word problem for each time. Partner up with a peer and solve each others word problems by putting the answer in the digital clock.

Example:

1:30

If Bridgit started reading her book at 1:30 and she read for 45 minutes, what time would it be when she stopped reading?

2:15

Analog	Digital	Word Problem	
	1:30		
	7:15		
	10:25		
	3:45		

Quiver Clocks Page
Time Conversion Practice
QuiverVision

Name: _____

Instructions: Call out a measurement of time and have students calculate a conversion. Start with hours to minutes, then go into minutes to seconds.

[21]

1	Hours	Minutes	2	Hours	Minutes	3	Hours	Minutes
4	Hours	Minutes	5	Hours	Minutes	6	Hours	Minutes
7	Hours	Minutes	8	Hours	Minutes	9	Hours	Minutes
10	Hours	Minutes	11	Minutes	Seconds	12	Minutes	Seconds
13	Minutes	Seconds	14	Minutes	Seconds	15	Minutes	Seconds
16	Minutes	Seconds	17	Minutes	Seconds	18	Minutes	Seconds
19	Minutes	Seconds	20	Minutes	Seconds	21	Minutes	Seconds

GRAPHING PARABOLAS

DESCRIPTION

In this activity students will watch and complete a Khan Academy lesson on parabolas. Afterwards, they will explore parabolas in real life via the arc of a basketball shot. Using the Quiver Vision 'Brian the Bull' coloring page, they will scan the page and take videos of their digital shots. Using Canva, they will place their videos behind a graph and draw a parabola and graph it.

This is activity is a great way to engage students with augmented reality and have them make real life connections to mathematical concepts.

LEARNING GOALS

- Students will be able to identify and recognize parabolas as the graphs of quadratic functions.
- Students will be able to define a parabola as the set of points which are all equidistant from the focus and directrix.

TEACHING TIPS

The parabola hyperdoc can be provided to students to explore this concept independently, or it can be used as support for students struggling with the process. A Desmos activity is embedded as well for extra practice.

DOK LEVEL ②

TYPE OF ASSIGNMENT

individual/Practice/Draw tool

GRADE LEVEL

8-12

STANDARDS

- CCSS.MATH.CONTENT.HSF.IF.C.7
Graph functions expressed symbolically and show key features of the graph, by hand in simple cases and using technology for more complicated cases.
- MM3G2.
Students will recognize, analyze, and graph the equations of the conic sections (parabolas, circles, ellipses, and hyperbolas). b. Graph conic sections, identifying fundamental characteristics.
- MM3P3.
Students will communicate mathematically. a. Organize and consolidate their mathematical thinking through communication. b. Communicate their mathematical thinking coherently and clearly to peers, teachers, and others.

ESSENTIAL QUESTIONS

- What do you notice about the shape of the graphs you've made?
- What kinds of functions have parabolas as their graphs?

APP INTEGRATIONS AND EXTENSIONS

QR CODE TO TEMPLATE

SCAN ME

ACTIVITIES

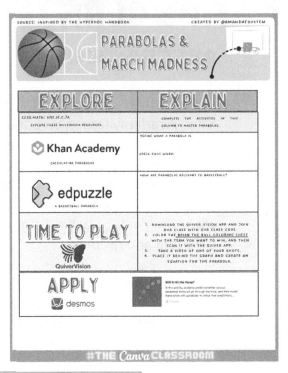

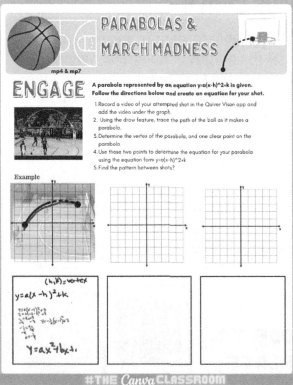

ENGAGE: SCAN THE PAGE AND PLAY BASKETBALL. TAKE A VIDEO OF YOUR SCREEN AS YOU PLAY AND ADD IT BEHIND THE GRAPH TO FIND THE PARABOLA.

TEMPLATES FOR LITTLES

TO ACCESS ALL THE TEMPLATES IN THIS SECTION
SCAN THE QR CODE OR GO TO THE WEBSITE BELOW.

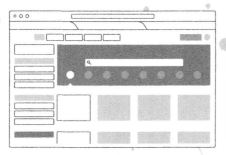

WWW.TEACHERGOALS.COM/CANVATEMPLATES

HANDWRITING PRACTICE

DESCRIPTION

Canva is great for creating learning materials for younger students to practice alphabet recall and handwriting practice. These worksheets are Markertown themed (a kid's book that can be found on Amazon and the read aloud is on youtube) and can be printed out, used digitally in SeeSaw, or even with the draw feature in Canva. This template includes access to all 26 letters of the alphabet and the numbers 1-10. There are a ton of other activities included in this template that aren't covered in this section, so be sure to check out the template!

LEARNING GOALS

- Students will learn and print the letters of the alphabet.
- Students will learn and print numbers 1-10.

TEACHING TIPS

When using this template digitally, you will want to assign it to students individually. With this age group I recommend uploading the practice handouts into another platform like SeeSaw or Flipgrid for students to practice. It includes arrows that show the path of motion their pencils should take when creating letters, as well as descriptions.

DOK LEVEL

TYPE OF ASSIGNMENT
Individual/Group

GRADE LEVEL
K-2

STANDARDS

While there are no Common Core Standards for teaching handwriting it is a common and. necessary practice in the earlier grades. Here are reasons to justify it:

Premise 1: Writing has a positive impact on the development of children's reading skills;
Premise 2: To derive this benefit, children have to engage in writing;
Premise 3: If they can write well (quickly, legibly), they will write more and better;
Premise 4: If children write more and better that will have a more positive impact on reading.

Source:
https://www.readingrockets.org/blogs/sh anahan-on-literacy/handwriting-time-common-core

ESSENTIAL QUESTIONS

- How does knowing how to write letters help me share my thoughts with others?
- Why is it important to learn how to write?

APP INTEGRATIONS AND EXTENSIONS

QR CODE TO TEMPLATE

SCAN ME

These handwriting templates also have students identify images that begin with the letter and the pages alternate to also prompt students to circle the capital and lowercase letters building letter recognition and phonics. The number pages provide students with an opportunity to count the items on the page. You don't have to use these specific templates. Customize your own to go with a theme of a book you are currently reading. There are also plenty of ready made templates searchable in Canva.

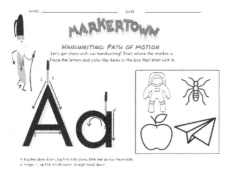
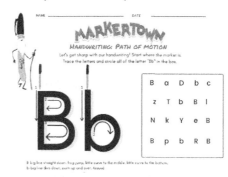

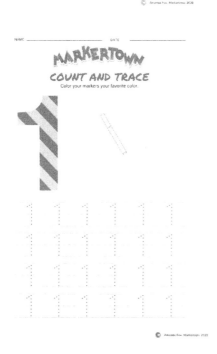

SENTENCE CONSTRUCTION

DESCRIPTION

This template teaches students basic sentence construction and provides the opportunity for handwriting practice, while learning to recognize written colors. This template is meant to be printed out for hands on application. Students will cut and paste the sentences in the correct syntax and color the markers the correct color that goes with the corresponding word.

DOK LEVEL 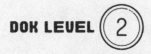 **②**

TYPE OF ASSIGNMENT

Individual/Hands on

GRADE LEVEL

K-1

STANDARDS

CCSS.ELA-LITERACY.L.K.1
Demonstrate command of the conventions of standard English grammar and usage when writing or speaking.

CCSS.ELA-LITERACY.L.K.1.F
Produce and expand complete sentences in shared language activities.

ESSENTIAL QUESTIONS

- What are the parts of a sentence?
- What are the colors of a rainbow?
- Why is it necessary to use different types of sentences while speaking and writing?

APP INTEGRATIONS AND EXTENSIONS

Canva

LEARNING GOALS

- Students will learn how to construct and assemble sentences.
- Students will practice color recognition.

TEACHING TIPS

This activity requires glue, scissors and print outs. It is not meant meant to be a digital lesson. In addition to handwriting, color, and sentence construction, it helps develop fine motor skills, hand strength, dexterity, and sequencing.

QR CODE TO TEMPLATE

SCAN ME

Print out these pages and provide them to students. The repetition of the word have and marker helps early readers. Being able to arrange the sentence in the correct order is an introductory skill for Kindergarteners and may be a refresher for first grade. Students also work on their dexterity and cutting and pasting skills. You can modify this template to create new sentences and even new sentence types. Instead of markers you can replace the item in the square.

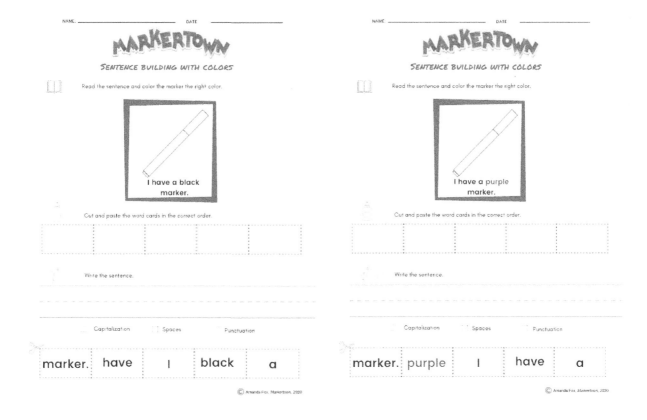

DIGITAL CODING

DESCRIPTION

This digital coding activity is great for younger students being introduced to coding. It features Stella, an alien trying to find her way back home. Students are prompted to drag and drop coding command arrows to demonstrate the shortest algorithm, or sequence of code. There are two levels that are built out, but you can duplicate and add more.

This activity is great for remote, hybrid, or in person learning. You can use this with an interactive whiteboard and have students try in front of the class, or assign it to each student individually.

LEARNING GOALS

- Students will learn what coding is.
- Students will drag and drop command arrows to build a coding sequence.

TEACHING TIPS

When using this template with students, you will want to lock everything on the game board except for the items (the arrows) that are meant to be draggable. This will prevent them from moving around other elements in the design, which could lead to frustration. If students complete the act of sequencing the code alone, it is a DOK 2, but when they are asked to reflect and complete the reflections activity it can ramp up the rigor to a level 3.

DOK LEVEL 2

TYPE OF ASSIGNMENT

Individual/Group

GRADE LEVEL

K-2

ISTE STANDARDS

5.1.a
Set professional learning goals to explore and apply teaching strategies for integrating CT practices into learning activities in ways that enhance student learning of both the academic discipline and CS concepts.

ESSENTIAL QUESTIONS

- How can I create the shortest sequence of code to get Stella home?
- What is an algorithm?
- What is a coding sequence?

APP INTEGRATIONS AND EXTENSIONS

Canva

QR CODE TO TEMPLATE

SCAN ME

This template can be customized to fit any theme you are currently covering in your class. It can be connected to history, literacy, or science. You could also have them code a fire escape plan to connect it to life skills and learning about fire safety. Have fun with it! Canva also has visual java script coding block templates that you could print out and use to have students build out sample code from projects in Cospaces or Scratch. They could even make a tutorial video on what each command means.

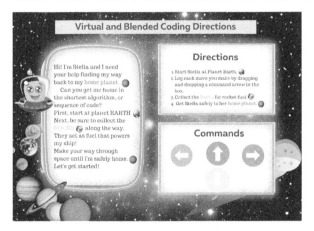
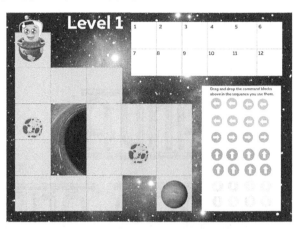

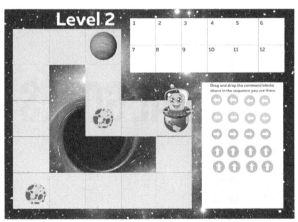
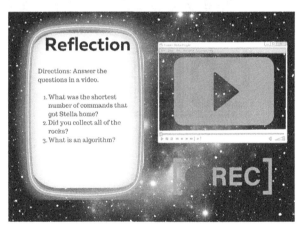

Board game Coding Blocks/Command Cards

Left   Forward   Right

Backward

CANVA, SDGS AND SCIENCE

THE GLOBAL GOALS

TO ACCESS ALL THE TEMPLATES IN THIS SECTION SCAN THE QR CODE OR GO TO THE WEBSITE BELOW.

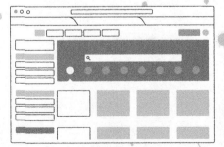

SCAN ME

WWW.TEACHERGOALS.COM/CANVATEMPLATES

GLOBAL GOALS + SCIENCE

DESCRIPTION

The United Nations created the Sustainable Development Goals in order to bring nations, communities, and the world together to solve world problems and make it a better place. You can bring the #GlobalGoals to your classroom as well with this template by introducing the 17 goals to students and then narrow down their focus to one or two goals. They can then identify a problem and pose a solution.

DOK LEVEL 4

TYPE OF ASSIGNMENT

Individual

GRADE LEVEL

K-12

STANDARDS

CSS.ELA-LITERACY.RI.
Ask and answer such questions as who, what, where, when, why, and how to demonstrate understanding of key details in a text.
CCSS.ELA-LITERACY.RI.
Describe the connection between a series of historical events, scientific ideas or concepts, or steps in technical procedures in a text.

Add content relevant standards here. I have used literacy across the curriculum.

ESSENTIAL QUESTIONS

- Which UN Global Goals interest you the most and why?
- Who are champions or activists for your goal?
- How can you take actions to help solve this problem locally? Globally?

APP INTEGRATIONS AND EXTENSIONS

Canva

LEARNING GOALS

- Students will research the 17 United Nations Sustainable Development Goals.
- Students will pose solutions to world problems through a local lens.
- Students will create a video or presentation communicating their research.

TEACHING TIPS

Begin by introducing students to the 17 Global Goals. Look at your curriculum to see what standards are relevant or make it a genius hour project. This particular project was created to be taught with Earth Day in mind. Students communicate their research using Flipgrid. You can have students add to our grid or create your own.

QR CODE TO TEMPLATE

📱 SCAN ME

GLOBAL GOALS INTRODUCTION ACTIVITY

Intro to Sustainable Development Goals

THE GLOBAL GOALS

Name: _____ Date: _____

Part Two:Research and summarize the goals.

Instructions: Research each of the 17 Sustainable Develop Goals, known as #globalgoals, and write one sentence to summarize each goal. You will pick one goal as the focus of your design challenge.

#THE *Canva*CLASSROOM

Intro to Sustainable Development Goals

Name: _____ Date: _____

Part Three: Planning Your Design

Instructions: Pick one #globalgoal to focus on for your design challenge. Answer the questions to help visualize your design. Use the space below to plan your design and sketch a prototype.

1. What is the issue the goal is trying to solve?

2. What visuals represent this issue?

3. What solutions or actions can we take in order to solve teh problem?

4. What visuals represent solutions?

#THE *Canva*CLASSROOM

Intro to Sustainable Development Goals

Name: _____ Date: _____

Instructions: While there are 17 #GlobalGoals, there are four that are related specifically to the environment. Explore the four goals listed below and write one sentence summarizing each goal.

Part Two: Research the goals listed below. You will pick one for the Earth Day Design challenge.

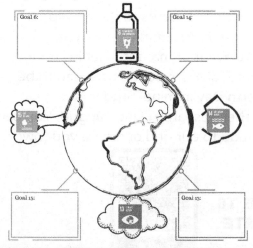

Goal 6:

Goal 14:

Goal 15:

Goal 13:

#THE *Canva*CLASSROOM

Intro to Sustainable Development Goals

Part Three: Planning Your Design

Instructions: Pick one #globalgoal as the focus of your design challenge. Answer the questions to help visualize your design. Use the space below to plan your design. Practice sketching your design in the circles.

1. What is the issue the goal is trying to solve?

2. What visuals represent this issue?

3. What solutions or actions can we take in order to solve the problem?

4. What visuals represent solutions?

Practice sketching out your globalgoal design in the circles before coloring on your AR Quiver sheet. .

#THE *Canva*CLASSROOM

In conjunction with Quiver Vision, the following SDG and Canva lesson plans were created with a focus on Earth Day. There are six main activities that you can implement in the science classroom; Earth Day and Global Goals, Life Below Water; Sea Turtles, Portrait of an Activist, and Life Above Land, and Mapping. Each of the templates have ancillary handouts, presentations, and lesson plans. The QR code to the master template is complete with links to videos, presentations, and ancillary lessons. The master template is included on the next page.

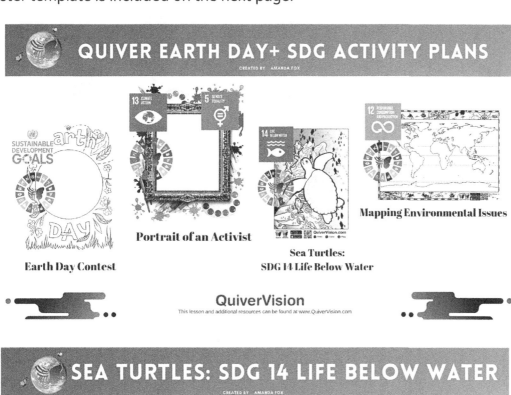

QUIVER EARTH DAY+ SDG ACTIVITY PLANS
CREATED BY AMANDA FOX

Earth Day Contest

Portrait of an Activist

Sea Turtles:
SDG 14 Life Below Water

Mapping Environmental Issues

QuiverVision
This lesson and additional resources can be found at www.QuiverVision.com

SEA TURTLES: SDG 14 LIFE BELOW WATER
CREATED BY AMANDA FOX

1 HOUR / K-5

ACTIVITY

TURTLE THREATS SLIDE DECK
GUIDED NOTES SHEET
AR COLORING PAGE

INTRO: Earth day is April 22, 2021 and was created to remind us to take care of the Earth. After watching the Quiver Earth day Video introduce students to pollution and life below water. Pollution and litter is a problem that our oceans face. Marine creatures, or creatures that live in the ocean like sea turtles and dolphins are put in danger from human debris. Watch the video on SDG 14 Life Below Water.

PART ONE: THREATS TO TURTLES

Sea turtles face threats that threaten their population and survival. Discuss the topics below with your students. Show them pictures using the Turtle Threats Slide Deck. How can we help solve this problem?

Plastic Debris
Entanglement
Global warming, Coral bleaching
Turtle shell jewelry

Plastic straw
Threats to turtle nests
Fishery by-catch

QuiverVision
This lesson and additional resources can be found at www.QuiverVision.com

EARTH DAY: PORTRAIT OF AN ACTIVIST

EARTH DAY: PORTRAIT OF AN ACTIVIST

CREATED BY AMANDA FOX

FREE

🕐 **2 HOURS** / 📖 **K-5**

STANDARDS

K-5 ACTIVIST SLIDES
K-2 COLOR, CUT, SORT
ACTIVIST VENN DIAGRAM
TEXT CONNECTIONS HANDOUT

Canva

K-5 ACTIVIST SLIDES
ACTIVIST VENN DIAGRAM
TEXT CONNECTIONS HANDOUT

PART ONE: Teacher Input

ACTIVITY

Intro: Earth Day is on April 22nd and is one of the biggest global holidays. The whole world comes together to protect our planet. The United Nations, a global organization that was formed to keep peace in the world, created a set of Global Goals to help us protect our planet. Goal #13 is climate action, and Goal 5 is Gender Equality. You are going to compare and contrast two activist who fight for two different causes trying to "Restore Earth". After you create a collage of an activist you will create a self portrait that represents how you can help solve these issues.

Use the Portrait of an Activist Slide deck to introduce students to Goal #13 and/or goal 5. Discuss with the class what an **activist** is. An **activist** is a person that helps bring about change. There are two options in this lesson; you can make this a biographical lesson or a Narrative Non-Fiction literacy/read aloud lesson. Go on to review Option A & B. (For 3-5 I recommend Option B).

QuiverVision

This lesson and additional resources can be found at www.QuiverVision.com

QR CODE TO SCIENCE LESSONS

📱 **SCAN ME**

STUDENT WORK SAMPLES

May 6
Kaye M 💬 0

May 6
CharlieC 💬 0

May 6
Molly J. 💬 0

May 5
Macy M. 💬 0

May 5
Eva M. 💬 0

May 5
Cameron H. 💬 0

May 5
Elizabeth W. 💬 0

May 5
Walton D. 💬 0

May 5
Amanda Nguyen 💬 0

May 5
Nicholas B. 💬 0

May 4
Vivianne G. 💬 0

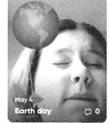

May 4
Earth day 💬 0

May 4
Anna S. 💬 0

May 4
Brock C. 💬 0

May 4
Raygan P. 💬 0

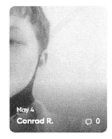

May 4
Conrad R. 💬 0

May 4
Peyton H. 💬 0

May 4
Kane H. 💬 0

May 4
Mason T. 💬 0

May 4
John H. 💬 0

JOIN CODE:
3AEB8BAF

SCAN ME

0:03 | 2:22   QuiverVision.com

Destination Six: Designing for Whole Galaxy

"THIS IS GROUND CONTROL TO MAJOR TOM
YOU'VE REALLY MADE THE GRADE
AND THE PAPERS WANT TO KNOW WHOSE
SHIRTS YOU WEAR
NOW IT'S TIME TO LEAVE THE CAPSULE IF
YOU DARE
THIS IS MAJOR TOM TO GROUND CONTROL
I'M STEPPING THROUGH THE DOOR
AND I'M FLOATING IN A MOST PECULIAR
WAY
AND THE STARS LOOK VERY DIFFERENT
TODAY."

"SPACE ODDITY" BY DAVID BOWIE

CONNECTING WITH CANVA

CONNECTING OUTSIDE OF THE CLASSROOM

As educators, building connections and relationships is one of the most important things that we do. Way before the first day of school we start planning our classroom environments, icebreakers, and even seek to connect with our students prior to the first day through phone calls, open houses, email, and even snail mail. The classroom is at the center of our day to day actions and the most important piece of our job, but we also need to be cognizant of the relationships and culture we cultivate in our entire educational galaxy. It is important to communicate with not only students, but also students' parents, administrators, grade level team members, virtual colleagues and even community members. Our success and our student's success depends on fostering positive relationships with all stakeholders. And when we do it well, new opportunities manifest themselves in forms we couldn't imagine. By design, Canva helps us connect and communicate in ways that are lightyears ahead of our predecessors.

MAKING SPACE FOR PARENT INVOLVEMENT

Making space for parents in our classroom isn't just about reporting about the weekly happenings to 'ground control' from your rocket ship of learning. With weekly communications, parents only have a planetary view of your classroom. But...there is way more to this relationship than providing a mere newsletter portal into your day to day grind. While keeping parents informed of each of their little star's progress ensures that you have a direct line to your biggest classroom supporters, it's also important to leave space for parental involvement. You don't want a negative interaction to be the first one you make. And let's face it! Parents are going to be the ones you call when issues arise in the classroom. So how can we use Canva to not only keep parents informed, but get them involved? In this section I'm going to cover several ways to not only keep parents informed, but get them involved in your classroom!

WEEKLY COMMUNICATION

Weekly communication in most schools is not only an expectation, but the bare minimum to involve parents in your classroom. My children's school sends home a Wednesday folder with any school happenings, updates, and records, but more and more students come from nontraditional households, or sometimes forget to check the folder. Some parents travel for work making it hard to have a united front when they don't always have access to the information. Doubling up on physical copies with a digital update allows you to reach parents on two fronts, while also delivering updates in a media that is convenient and they may prefer. Having a consistent delivery day also helps, as parents will know to look for an email or update. Emails are a great 'green' way to summarize what is going on in your classroom each week and they also allow you to add content such as student work, and video updates, which are either impossible or cumbersome with printed materials. With Canva you can create a weekly planning template that can be replicated and shared directly in your email via link. They even integrate into Mailchimp!

You can curate and archive these newsletters for reference using a platform like Wakelet, and including one link to all past previous communications in your email signature. Setting up expectations and procedures early sets a good foundation for the year. With parents, there is no such thing as over communicating! Here is a sample Wakelet newsletter that our Jr. High team sent home each week to parents.

Holy Trinity Jr High Newsletter

All newsletter will be collected here, with the most recent one at the top

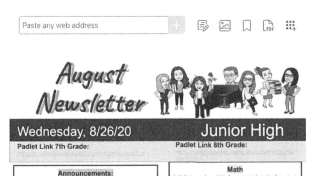

Canva made it easy for our team to work asynchronously on our weekly content. You just share an edit link with all members of your team and they can add what they want to for the week. This was important since we all had different planning periods. We sent the Wakelet link via Remind, an educational communication platform, and also added it to our email signature. Any Canva links, student work, or forms could also be added to the Wakelet so parents only had to reference one spot!

You can also create a Wakelet of student work and embed the link in your newsletter Wakelet!

PARENT AND STAKEHOLDER INVOLVEMENT

Parent Involvement

There are so many opportunities for parents and stakeholders to get involved in your classroom by contributing to Canva designs. Think holidays, birthdays, start student of the week! Below I'm going to share some awesome ideas to invite parents and community stakeholders to contribute to your classroom culture!

Back to School Video Message from Parents

I have been greeted at open house or the first day of school with the opportunity to write a letter describing my kiddos. Usually, it comes in the form of a blank piece of paper with instructions to write a few paragraphs describing my child without naming them to help the teacher get to know the students in the room and build community. You can do this digitally via Canva! Want to take the assignment up a notch? Have parents leave video messages of what they hope their first day of school is like. This can help with littles who may be a little homesick, while also creating an opportunity to celebrate the unique interests of the students in the room! It's also a good way to put a face and name to parents!

Star Student Video

Every week at my daughter's school, a student of the week is celebrated. Create a video presentation template where parents can fill out the same interest survey their child does. Compare the students responses to the parent/guardian responses and include an opportunity for relatives to celebrate the student as well!

Birthday Message

Create a video presentation for each student and share the edit link via a QR code. Post these on an interactive bulletin board and allow other students, teachers, parents, and faculty to add to the presentation. On that students birthday play the presentation for the rest of the class, or put it in a card for the student to take home!

Senior Tributes

Senior year of high school calls for celebrations, and also senior tributes. Create a video presentation QR board in the hallway or school communal space and have faculty, students, and other members of the community pay them tribute prior to graduation. Videos, gifs, and text tributes can all be added and it will be a keepsake students can add to their yearbooks. Using video is a nice personal touch to honor students on this occasion!

The Masked Reader

Have community members and school faculty that are well known add a video of them reading a book to your class. The video should just be of the book, and they can add a photo of themselves masked to the template. Let students have fun trying to find out who The Masked Reader is that week! Check out the example!

QR CODE TO
MASKED READER

THE SOCIAL MEDIA UNIVERSE

Today, social media is a given. In regards to my teaching and classroom, it has been one of the most amazing ways I have been able to connect my classroom with parents, community members, and businesses. I started using twitter in 2012, and since then I have had so many wonderful professional connections that helped me sharpen my pedagogical craft, and also connect me with community stakeholders that have become involved in speaking to my students, funding film festival scholarships, and even in creating opportunities to share my work in person via workshops and conferences. I have also used Facebook to connect with parents and help spread the word of school events like ComicCons, Gaming Arcades, and STEM Movie Nights.

Recently, I adopted Instagram to share fun classroom happenings. I also share my professional work on Linkedin in order to share tutorial videos and posts to a professional audience in order to grow my online presence. You never know the next opportunity that is out there! If you aren't using social media for educational purposes I highly recommend starting now!

Canva has made it even easier to create aesthetic and engaging content with ease. The platform has social media dimensions built in and takes the guesswork out of pixel sizes and formats making it a time saving go to! Designing graphics for your school or classroom social media universe and even your classroom newsletter has never been more intuitive or time efficient. And what's even better...there is a built in planner to help you create content and schedule it! Most recently, Canva added the Bobcaat social media planner to help schedule and push posts to multiple channels.

SCHEDULE POSTS TO THE FOLLOWING PLATFORMS:

HOW TO SHARE POSTS ON SOCIAL (PULLED FROM CANVA)

1. On the Canva homepage side menu, click Content Planner.
2. Next to when you want to schedule the post, click on the plus icon.
3. Select to schedule an existing design, or create a new design to schedule.
4. Scheduling existing designs: Under 'recent designs', select which one you want to schedule. If it's not there, click on 'your projects' to search for it. Click to select it.
5. Creating designs to schedule: Click on 'create a design.' Select the design that you want to create, or use the search bar. To schedule it, click Share on the menu above the editor, and select 'schedule.' If it's not there, click on 'more first.'
6. On the schedule window next to the date, click on the icon to change the time and date, to edit the design, and for more options. The time follows your local time zone.
7. Click 'select a channel,' and select the social media account that you want to schedule the post to. If there's no connected account yet, click 'connect,' and log into the account that you want to use.
8. If your design has multiple pages, select the pages that you want to publish. The number of pages and design export size depend on social media limitations. See 'social media export limits' for details.
9. Write a caption if you want, and click 'schedule post' to finish.

Currently, you can only schedule a design to one social media post.

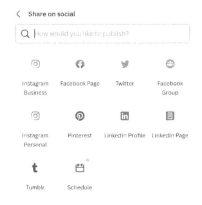

SCAN QR CODE TO LEARN MORE ABOUT SCHEDULING POSTS

SIZE UP YOUR SOCIAL MEDIA DESIGN SIZES

Designing graphics can be confusing when it comes to pixels, dimensions, and size, and each platform calls for a different format. So, you want to create your social media graphics from scratch? Consider the following tables as a quick design size reference for creating custom graphics for social media! Simply go to 'create new design' select 'custom size' and put in the correct pixels for each design. Take the guess work out when designing your templates!

TYPE	SIZE
Channel Icon	800 × 800 px
Channel Art	2,560 × 1,440 px
Desktop Display	2,560 × 423 px
Tablet Display	1,855 × 423 px
Desktop and Mobile Display	1,546 × 423 px
Video Thumbnail	1,280 × 720 px

TYPE	SIZE
Profile Picture	180 × 180 px
Cover Photo	820 × 312 px
Image Post	1,200 × 630 px
Shared Link Images	1,200 × 628 px
Tab Images	111 × 74 px
Event Image	1,200 × 1,080 px
Facebook Ad	1,200 × 628 px

TYPE	SIZE
Header Photo	1,500 × 500 px
Profile Photo	400 × 400 px
Twitter Post	1,024 × 512 px
Cards Image	800 × 320 px
Summary Card Image	280 × 150 px

TYPE	SIZE
Profile Photo	110 × 110 px
Square Images	1,080 × 1,080 px
Images	1,080 × 1,350 px
Stories	1,080 × 1,920 px

TYPE	SIZE
Profile Photo	400 × 400 px
Cover Photo	1,584 × 396 px
Shared Image	180 × 110 px

TYPE	SIZE
Profile Photo	400 × 400 px
Cover Photo	1,584 × 396 px
Shared Image	180 × 110 px

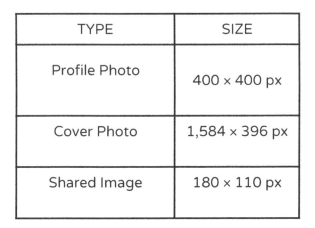

EDUCATOR CREATOR

By this point in the book, I hope you feel like you have a good grasp on design. It may be time to take it to the next level and share your amazing work with other educators in Canva and get paid. If you are there, you should sign up for the Education Creators program! This is a new initiative within Canva that allows teachers to create, publish and earn from their educational templates on Canva.

The program was launched in June of 2020 and allows educators to share their made-from-scratch custom templates with other educators. All you have to do is design educational resources that reflect your teaching style, publish your designs, and sit back and earn each time an educator uses your template.

You must sign up and be accepted before you are provided with a creator account. All designs must be remixable for other educators to use, and go through a review process before they are approved.

Creators are paid via a royalty model on the 15th of each month and royalties are based on how many pro Canva templates are exported. Sign up today!

SCAN QR CODE TO SIGN UP TO BECOME AN EDUCATOR CREATIVE!

MADE IN *Canva*

CANVA MONTHLY EDTECH ROUNDUP

BY STACEY ROSHAN

At the end of each month, I put out a roundup of tips that I've shared with faculty at my school in the four weeks preceding. I use Canva to create a visually appealing graphic highlighting tips and tutorials for review and easy access. Additionally, I include a shout-out to a project or lesson created by one of our teachers inspired by a tech tip. In this way, teachers can be energized by ideas their colleagues have brought to life and see the tips in action as we celebrate innovative teaching and learning.

I choose Canva to create my monthly roundup for several reasons. First, I love the templates. I enjoy choosing something new each month knowing that it won't entail a lot of time spent designing on my end. The font choices, color options, built-in shapes and graphics are all reasons I love creating in Canva. Additionally, I can embed content from a variety of sites. This can be helpful in both making things more visually appealing and also to improve the reader experience. I choose to embed content that I think many people will want to review, and I use hyperlinks for other reference material to reduce visual clutter.

Another standout feature of Canva is the built-in QR code generator. I have used Canva for a variety of visual displays at my school and printed with the poster printer we have. For the monthly edtech roundup I have described, this is something that can be printed on standard paper and hung in high traffic places, like by the faculty copier. You could either:

1. include just one QR code on the Canva poster — when scanned, this would open the Canva on the teacher's phone with clickable hyperlinks and embedded content; or
2. include QR codes for highlighted content so that teacher's can scan the QR code and open the tip directly.

Here are instructions to execute each of those options.

SCAN TO COPY DESIGN

SCAN TO WATCH VIDEO

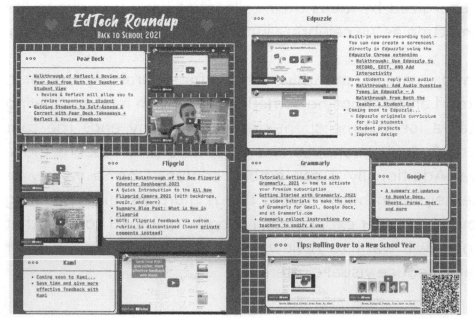

TEMPLATE THAT INSPIRED THE DESIGN

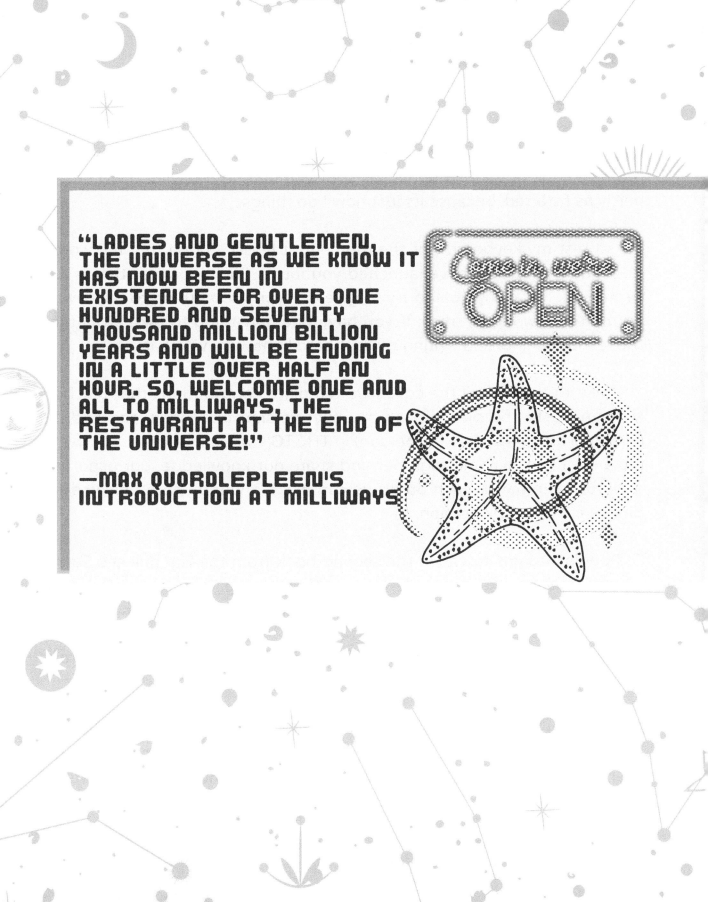

"LADIES AND GENTLEMEN, THE UNIVERSE AS WE KNOW IT HAS NOW BEEN IN EXISTENCE FOR OVER ONE HUNDRED AND SEVENTY THOUSAND MILLION BILLION YEARS AND WILL BE ENDING IN A LITTLE OVER HALF AN HOUR. SO, WELCOME ONE AND ALL TO MILLIWAYS, THE RESTAURANT AT THE END OF THE UNIVERSE!"

—MAX QUORDLEPLEEN'S INTRODUCTION AT MILLIWAYS

AFTERWORD

Here we are friends. We are at the end of our journey…or are we? Either way, I want to welcome you to the restaurant at the end of the universe. I promise none of your students will spot you here in the wild…I will end as nerdy as I started, because its just how I do things.

As I rest my keyboard (for the moment at least), I hope that my words, ideas, and templates have launched you into a Canva journey that is just beginning. It was my goal to try to give everyone something to take away, no matter how big or small. If you have one new thing to take away then the restless nights and writing by keyboard light were worth it.

I like to think of all the collective template contributions that teachers have made to the platform as our own version of Marvin, the android (though I am more of a Mac person) in THGTG's who has a brain the size of a planet. If we all come together and share our knowledge, our expertise, and our talents with each other we can make a world—no a universe—of difference to our profession.

Douglas Adams taunts in the second book from the Hitchhiker's Series, "if you've done six impossible things this morning, why not round it off with breakfast at Milliways, the Restaurant at the End of the Universe."

Teaching can sometimes feel like an impossible job and like there is always more that we could be doing—if we just but had the time.

Canva helps give us time back with the robust reservoir of templates, letting us focus on what truly matters: the students. We do the impossible everyday. We continue for our students. We are not just designers of templates, or lessons. We help the future generations of tomorrow design their destinies.

The restaurant at the end of the universe in The Hitchhiker's Guide to the Galaxy Series is where book two picks up. And I promise you there will be a book two in the Hitchhiker's Guide for Educators Series. There are already a few in the works! As I reflect with my Earthly version of a Pan Galactic Gargleblaster I want to thank you for your patronage to my menu of templates and hope they spawn an appetite to create.

"CURIOUSLY ENOUGH, THE DOLPHINS HAD LONG KNOWN OF THE IMPENDING DEMOLITION OF EARTH AND HAD MADE MANY ATTEMPTS TO ALERT MANKIND TO THE DANGER. BUT MOST OF THEIR COMMUNICATIONS WERE MISINTERPRETED AS AMUSING ATTEMPTS TO PUNCH FOOTBALLS, OR WHISTLE FOR TITBITS, SO THEY EVENTUALLY GAVE UP AND LEFT THE EARTH BY THEIR OWN MEANS - SHORTLY BEFORE THE VOGONS ARRIVED. THE LAST EVER DOLPHIN MESSAGE WAS MISINTERPRETED AS A SURPRISINGLY SOPHISTICATED ATTEMPT TO DO A DOUBLE BACKWARDS SOMERSAULT THROUGH A HOOP, WHILST WHISTLING THE 'STAR-SPANGLED BANNER'. BUT, IN FACT, THE MESSAGE WAS THIS "SO LONG AND THANKS FOR ALL THE FISH".

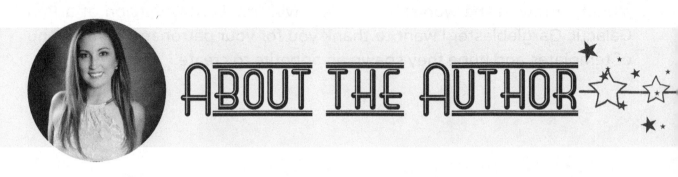

ABOUT THE AUTHOR

Amanda Fox is an award winning teacher and Savannah, Georgia native who currently lives and works in Prospect, Kentucky. She is the Chief Content Officer for TeacherGoals. Recipient of the 2016 ISTE Emerging Leader Award, recognized as a PBS Digital innovator for her initiatives in enhancing student learning with technology, Fox has also served as President of the Young Educator Network for ISTE, and received the President's Volunteer Award.

She is author of The Hitchhiker's Guide to the Canva Classroom, Teachingland, Zom-Be a Design Thinker, and the Markertown Series. Her inspiration for Markertown came from her kids Rowan, Bridgit, Connor, and Finn, who are constantly giving her ideas for new stories and adventures to inspire the world. She believes caps should always be put back on markers, and toothpaste, but never Mexican cokes. Learn more or connect with Amanda on Twitter @AmandaFoxSTEM or via email at amanda@teachergoals.com.

For more information on booking Amanda for book readings, summer camps, keynotes, workshops, design thinking led sessions, or video conferencing/virtual book readings with your class or school, go to teachergoals.com/pd.

For awesome classroom content and activities for Markertown, check out teachergoals.com/markertown!

Cultivate Canva Classrooms in Your District

#THECANVACLASSROOM WORKSHOP

How can you leverage Canva to its fullest potential to cultivate the 4 C's in your district, while also saving time, but not sacrificing rigor? With Canva, lessons can be pretty AND powerful! In this session or workshop Amanda will share classroom tested templates and strategies and unlock hidden tips to boost not only teacher engagement, but also student outcomes. Reach out to contact@teachergoals.com to book Amanda for a transformative professional development experience that will have everyone believing they can, can, can.

#THECANVACLASSROOM KEYNOTE

In this fun and engaging keynote, chocked full of pop culture references, educators are invited to hitchhike their way through a beautifully designed universe of templates that span all content and grade levels. Built on the foundation of DOK, UDL, and UBD teachers will walk away inspired and grounded in good pedagogy. Amanda will share her educational journey and the dreams for what education could and should be.

PROFESSIONAL DEVELOPMENT OFFERINGS

For more information on booking Amanda for book readings, summer camps, keynotes, workshops, design thinking led sessions, or video conferencing/virtual book readings with your class or school, go to Teachergoals.com. If you are looking for an asynchronous PD credited course check out her Canva Classroom online offering through TeacherGoals.com/courses. Amanda can customize and tailor school and district trainings to fit your specific need as well.

@ AMANDAFOXSTEM

SESSIONS AND WORKSHOPS

CANVA VISION: VIDEO CREATION FOR MULTIVERSE INSTRUCTION

DOK PUNCHOUT: TKO DOK WITH CANVA

THE CANVA CLASSROOM VIRTUAL COURSE BY TEACHERGOALS

OH SNAP: APP SMASHING IN THE CANVA UNIVERSE

THE HITCHHIKER'S GUIDE TO THE CANVA CLASSROOM

STRANGER PEDAGOGY: TURNING CLASSROOM INSTRUCTION UPSIDE DOWN

TEACHERGOALS.COM/PD   CONTACT@TEACHERGOALS.COM

 COURSES *by* TEACHERGOALS

REGISTER NOW!

www.teachergoals.com/canvaclassroomcourse

Don't panic! Relax, because this course, based on *The Canva Classroom* book is designed as an educator's design guide to creating meaningful student tasks and projects using the Canva design platform. Each module is designed to help you fully leverage the Canva platform with the goal of embracing creativity, student voice, collaboration, critical thinking, and community. With over 8 hours of video enhanced instruction you are guaranteed to walk away a Canva pro!

01 Canva for Education Set Up

02 Designing For Inclusivity: UbD and UDL

03 Designing for Depth of Knowledge

04 Using Canva to Enhance Instruction

05 Canva Tips, Hacks, and Tricks

06 Canva App Integrations and App Smashing

07 Creating a Canva Brand Kit

08 Creating Learning Experiences in Canva

09 Feedback, Assessment, and Folders

10 Social Media and Community Building

PARTICIPANTS WILL:

- Learn how to set up a Canva Classroom and register for the Canva Education Dashboard.
- Explore pedagogical foundations such as Depth of Knowledge, Universal Design Framework, Backwards Design.
- Explore over 10 ways to app smash with Canva and be given examples.
- Complete learning tasks demonstrating understanding of Canva feature and functions.
- Experience the platform from a student perspective.
- Create a classroom, school, or district brand kit.
- Design an interactive lesson using Canva and its integrated functions.
- Learn how to organize folders, follow creators, and save elements.
- Explore multiple ways to provide feedback and assessment using Canva.
- Learn how to use Canva to engage socially and build a global PLN.
- Interact with other Canva Educators in the FB Group.

ACKNOWLEDGEMENTS

I would like to specially thank Erik Francis, Eric Curts, Tara Hannon, Michael Cohen, Michael Harvey, Arlene Soto, and Brett Salakas for providing invaluable feedback during my author journey. You guys have been my sound board and I appreciate the time and feedback provided to make this book what it is.

I would also like to thank the educators that contributed to the book by adding their Canva experiences and templates for readers to digest: Erik Francis, Ryan Read, Tisha Richmond, Heather Brown, Stacey Roshan, Alex Isaacs, Colby Hawkins, and Melissa Sullivan. An extra shout out to Heather Brown for taking the time to read through the whole text and give me editing advice page for page.

I was also amazed at the response when I asked for help with the book launch. Special shout out and thanks to those that volunteered to review, provide feedback, and help spread the word about The Canva Classroom: Keven Rinaman, Megan Trahan, Ashley Parker, Nadine Gilkison, Megan Bengs, Sarah Margeson, Dahlia Sirilla, Cheyenne Kolody, Laura Parenti, Sherry Potter, Michael Harvey, Renee Dawson, Ryan Read, Danae Acker, Heather Brown, Chad Behnke, Lisa Stull, Lizbeth Morales Menendez, Shozo Suzuki, Lyneth Crighton, Leslie Brophy, Barbara Ramirez, Kim Voge, Kathy O'Dowd, Alejandra Lopez, Melody McAllister, Megan Heineman, Hollie Sisk, Melissa Layton, Penny Roadley, Elena Vercher, Shannon Bynum, Stacy Kratochvil, Nicole Tschappat, Paula Ott, Taylor Ray, Bobby Brian Lewis, Alex Chaucer, Thurndotte Ray, Catherine Coleman, and Natalie Miller. An old African proverb says, "Go fast alone, or farther together." Thank you for helping me go far, and being willing to be part of this journey.

Last, but not least, thank you, reader. Without you I wouldn't have been inspired to write this guide, and I hope that you find your own inspiration as you thumb the pages. May you enjoy your launch into a Canva journey that transforms your classroom and helps students reach their full potential.

So long, and thanks for all the fish, Amanda Fox

REFERENCES

42. (n.d.). Hitchhikers. Retrieved December 7, 2021, from
https://hitchhikers.fandom.com/wiki/42

Adams, D. (n.d.). The Hitchhiker's Guide to the Galaxy. sparknotes.
https://www.sparknotes.com/lit/hitchhikers-guide-to-the-galaxy/summary/

Aungst, G. (2014, September 4). Using Webb's Depth of Knowledge to Increase
Rigor. edutopia. https://www.edutopia.org/blog/webbs-depth-knowledge-
increase-rigor-gerald-aungst

Brodsky, J. (2020, December 29). Why Questioning Is The Ultimate Learning Skill.
Forbes. https://www.forbes.com/sites/juliabrodsky/2021/12/29/why-
questioning-is-the-ultimate-learning-skill/?sh=839fe1c399fe

Canva. (n.d.-a). App smash Canva and ThingLink to make your designs
interactive
and engaging. https://www.canva.com/learn/app-smash-canva-and-
thinglink -make-designs-interactive/

Canva. (n.d.-b). Design elements and principles.
https://www.canva.com/learn/design-elements-principles/

Carnegie Mellon University. (n.d.). What is the difference between formative and
summative assessment
https://www.cmu.edu/teaching/assessment/basics/formative
summative.html#:~:text=The%20goal%20of%20formative%2
0assessment,target%20areas%20that%20need%20work

CAST. (2020). Key Questions to Consider When Planning Lessons.
https://www.cast.org/products-services/resources/2020/udl-guidelines-key-
questions-planning-lessons

Create digital worksheets. (n.d.). Wizer.me. Retrieved January 28, 2022 from
    https://app.wizer.me/

Delahaye, J.-P. (2020, September 21). THE Sciences for Math Fans: A
    Hitchhiker's Guide to the Number 42. Scientific American.
    https://www.scientificamerican.com/article/for-math-fans-a-hitchhikers
    guide-to-the-number-42/

Dunstan, J. (2018, July 4). The answer to Life, The Universe and Everything is
    42 ... but why 42? The Coast. https://www.thecoast.net.nz/shows/drive
    with-jon-dunstan/the-answer-to-life-the-universe-and-everything-is-42
    but-why-42/?fbclid=IwAR1kjd5a9ic9Q_p6M-RJ-
    JANK_BEGAoUKcOCNgtwrZxXBJ8XLR

EDPuzzle Staff. (2019, June 18). What is app smashing? EDTECH.
    https://blog.edpuzzle.com/edtech/app-smashing/

Francis, E. (Host). (2020, February 18). How to Promote Cognitive Rigor
    Through Classroom Questioning (No. 41) [Audio podcast episode]. In
    PodBean. https://andreasamadi.podbean.com/e/ascd-author-erik-
    francis-on-how-to-use-questions-to-promote-cognitive-rigor-
    thinking-and-learning/

Heroes, A. (2015, September 5). The Principles of Design YouTube.
    https://www.youtube.com/watch?v=ZK86XQ1iFVs

Pluralsight. (2015, January 19). How to Read Hex Color Codes.
    Pttps://www.pluralsight.com/blog/tutorials/understanding-hexadecimal-
    colorssimple#:~:text=Hex%20color%20codes%20are%20one,as%20hexa
    decimal%20color%20or%20hex.&text=The%20color%20values%20are%2
    0defined,value%20is%20higher%20than%209

Shanahan, T. (2014, September 24). Handwriting in the Time of Common Core. Reading Rockets. https://www.readingrockets.org/blogs/shanahan on-literacy/handwriting-time-common-core

Spencer, J. (2020, September 23). Using Scavenger Hunts to Get Students Moving in Virtual Learning. John Spencer. https://spencerauthor.com/scavenger-hunts/

The UDL Guidelines. (n.d.). Cast. Retrieved January 20, 2022 from https://udlguidelines.cast.org/

Walkup, J. R. (2013, December 25). Bad DOK Chart Sabotages Understanding of Depth of Knowledge. Cognitive Rigor to the core! http://cognitiverigor.blogspot.com/2014/04/by-john-r.html

Webb's Depth of Knowledge Guide: Career and Technical Education Definitions. (2009). CCREA.net. Retrieved December 29, 2021 from http://www.ccresa.net/wp-content/uploads/2012/06/Webbs-DOK Guide.pdf

Wiggins, G., Wiggins, G. P., & McTighe, J. (2005). Understanding by design (2nd ed.). ASCD

MORE FROM

TEACHERGOALS PUBLISHING

MARKERTOWN
BY AMANDA FOX

After a long day of coloring, the markers are heading home to their boxes—but Glitter can't find her cap! As Glitter journeys through Markertown she meets a group of repurposed markers that help her envision a different future. But can they save her ink in time?

Markertown, is a story that commends kindness and friendship. It embraces upcycling not only markers, but parts of ourselves along our journey. Readers should walk away understanding that true sparkle and shine come from within. So let the mark you leave on the world be one of kindness!

With nods to Van Gogh's Starry Night, vibrant whimsical pages, and interactive augmented reality coloring pages, Markertown is the perfect gift for children, teachers, back-to-school, or any time of year! Perfect for fans of The Day the Crayons Quit by Drew Deywalt and Not Just A Scribble by Diane Albers.

THE QUIVER CLASSROOM
THE HITCHHIKER'S GUIDE FOR EDUCATORS SERIES
BY TARA HANNON AND AMANDA FOX

Augmented reality (AR) has been shown to have good potential in making the learning process more active, effective and meaningful
The book:
- Provides 42 common core, ISTE, and Next generation science standard aligned step-by-step lessons created to seamlessly integrate augmented reality in your classroom.
- Includes interactive content, with more than 42 pages that can be scanned in order to experience augmented reality!
- Comes with a network of augmented reality experts to join and learn from online!

MY FIRST AUGMENTED REALITY WORKBOOK SERIES
BY TEACHERGOALS

TeacherGoals Publishing is an educational publishing company that is set on disrupting the way kids learn, read, and develop literacy skills. Check out our student workbooks that come enhanced with augmented reality. Augmented reality overlays digital content and information onto the physical world, in this instance, digital content that explains, instructs, and even guides students through skill-building. Kids can unlock this content by downloading the Quiver app and scanning the pages. When scanned, the pages come to life and leave kids wanting to revisit the books again and again. For bulk purchasing for classrooms or schools please contact us at publishing@teachergoals.com.

THE CANUA CLASSROOM SERIES

THE CANUA SCHOOL
THE HITCHHIKER'S GUIDE FOR EDUCATORS SERIES
BY DANAE ACKER & DR. JOHN WICK

The Canva School picks up where The Canva Classroom finished. Reaching beyond the classroom this book will take a look at a systems approach to Canva implementation and how this tool can be leveraged to make leading, teaching, and learning easier and more efficient.Join forces with two incredible innovative thought leaders in the world of educational technology (Principal John Wick, and Digital Integration Specialist Danae Acker) as they guide you through the process of setting up a Canva ecosystem that works for small schools, large schools, private schools, and public schools. Learn from their experiences and journey in establishing Canva as one of the main components of school operations and vitality.   You will gain access to useful templates, workflows, and resources that will make you wonder how you ever survived during the PC years (Prior to Canva).

THE CANUA CLASSROOM MATH EXPANSION PACK
THE HITCHHIKER'S GUIDE FOR EDUCATORS SERIES
BY HEATHER BROWN AND AMANDA FOX

This spin-off of the best-selling book, The Canva Classroom, focuses on sparking the love of math in students from kindergarten through high school. While most adults have experienced math anxiety at least at one point, this book will help to alleviate that anxiety for students and have them craving more math time! It goes beyond the standards commonly focused on in math and delves into the standards of mathematical processes which increase important life skills such as critical thinking and perseverance, and skills that every teacher dreams of instilling into their students.

THE CANUA CLASSROOM LITERACY EXPANSION PACK
THE HITCHHIKER'S GUIDE FOR EDUCATORS SERIES
BY KRISTINA HOLZWEISS

In our Literacy Expansion Pack Kristina covers Canva for Research, Reading, and Writing. It is filled with templates and ideas to support literacy for students of all ages and ability levels. Learn how to develop lessons, activities, and assessments that will increase student engagement and understanding of a variety of text formats. With Canva, your students will have an accessible "on-ramp" to creating projects such as book bentos, comics, and visual memoirs that combine multimedia elements including text, images, videos, and audio.

THE CANUA CLASSROOM SOCIAL STUDIES EXPANSION PACK
THE HITCHHIKER'S GUIDE FOR EDUCATORS SERIES
BY KATHERINE GOYETTE AND ADAM JUAREZ

Our fourth book in our Canva Series focuses on project-based design in the social studies classroom. In this book you will learn to use Canva to engage students as active consumers and creators of content in Social Studies, in concert with English Language Arts common core literacy standards. Motivate students to read, write, listen, and speak about Social Studies content via media rich templates made with today's learner in mind.

THE CANUA GLOSSARY FOR EDUCATION: CANUA A TO Z
THE HITCHHIKER'S GUIDE FOR EDUCATORS SERIES
BY AMANDA FOX

New to Canva? Canva from A to Z was written to be your quick reference guide to getting started quickly with Canva! If your school has caught the #CANVALOVE bug then chances are you in need of this guide to help navigate the dashboard, explore the app integrations and learn about all the features Canva has to offer you and your students!

UPCOMING EDUCATION TITLES

THE SCIENCE OF READING IN ACTION
BY MALIA HOLOWELL

LOGICAL DISCIPLINE
BY BRAD WEINSTEIN,
NATHAN MAYNARD,
AND DR. LUKE ROBERTS

HEARTLEADER
BY MATTHEW J. BOWERMAN

UPCOMING CHILDREN'S BOOKS

MONSTERS HAVE MANNERS
BY JEFF KUBIAK

PETER O' METER
BY TRICIA FUGLESTAD

THE SNOW FLURRY FAIRY
BY TRICIA FUGLESTAD

FOR MORE INFORMATION ON OUR AUTHORS AND BOOK CATALOGUE GO TO
WWW.TEACHERGOALS.COM/AUTHORS

Made in United States
Orlando, FL
12 April 2024